The Adventures of Bamo

THE ADVENTURES OF BAMO

From Struggles and Pains to Hopes and Gains

Keleti Sanon

Mandingo Publishing
Humble, TX

The Adventures of Bamo: From Struggles and Pains to Hopes and Gains

Copyright © 2018 by Keleti Sanon

Published by Mandingo Publishing
Cover Design by Rodney Steven Pate
Author Photograph Evelyn Maria Photography

ISBN: 10: 0-578-43111-4
ISBN-13: 978-0-578-43111-6

Revised Edition: June 2020

DEDICATION

This book is dedicated to my mother, Diaka Toure, and all the children in the world, without borders.

As a child, I felt your love for our family—husband, kids and neighbors—was unlimited. Your struggles during the sickness that took your life away to heaven and left me and my siblings here at a very young age is a lifetime memory for me. The love you showed me carried me across many obstacles from Africa to the United States of America.

I remember all that happened in Oume at the family house at my young age of six and up and also whenever I visited your side of the family from Abidjan. Those were the best times.

You were a mother of strength, dedicated to love and saving your family by any means with class in our impoverished life, where we didn't even have a meal every day.

I remember you boiling just water in the communal kitchen in the compound, so your family didn't get picked on because we didn't have anything to eat, while I and my siblings and dad were all in pain of hunger.

You protected my father during his horrible and painful sickness over the years that finally took his life a few years after you departed.

You were a mother of LOVE, courage, attitudes, strength, and belief that one day, life would be better for either all or some of us your kids.

Thanks, Mom. Some of us departed to join you, but the rest of us are still behind and still in the fight with life, but in a different manner—better.

Just know, we love each other as you taught us and support each other nonstop—and we will not stop.

Your children are today, all men and women, as life expected. The children of this world experience so many situations either good or bad. They have so much love to offer each other without border because they are just seeing the connection in their spirit and soul, but not in the physical body that carries them.

My childhood was so well cared for by you—even in our deep level of poverty—that I will always support children around the world.

Thank you, Mom! We all are well!!! And missing you all the time.

Keleti Sanon

About the Cover Art

The cover depicts a typical day in the village of Oume. Bamo, the main character is at the center of the village at the Baobab tree and one of his mothers that raised him is there with him.

The Baobab tree depicted in the picture is a central symbol in the village. Many important and significant events, announcements, and gatherings occur around this tree. The tree represents refuge as depicted by the older man taking rest under the shade of the tree. It represents a place of gathering and counseling as depicted by the mothers giving their children daily affirmations before sending them off to walk to the town school many miles away. The birds flying around and sitting on the tree represent the presence of nature that God controls for living creatures to enjoy. There are several paths to reach the farm or visit other neighbors as depicted by the lady with the head basket. The goat and chickens are a part of everyday village life as it is their home as well.

ACKNOWLEDGEMENTS

People in our life come and go and everyone comes into our life to serve a purpose. That purpose will either be revealed to us immediately or some time later in life. It may be good or bad, but it all ends up in the positive and meaningful recipe that composes our life. The following people have had an impact on my life at a certain point during my growth and their impact continues to create growth in my life. They deserve a special thanks for all they've meant to me and for the gift has created them to be in my life. Their portion of the recipe made me who I am today. I am so very thankful and appreciative of them.

New York: Kaba Sano, Keyanni Griffith, Moussa Sanogo (Baba), Warren Wright, Diaka Sano, Gnale Sano, Tracey Collins, Irving Codrington.

North Carolina: Blanche Penn, Krystal Bell, Jay Bell, Marcus Johnson, Sr., Nail Johnson, Ressie Johnson, Barbara Johnson, Lacy Johnson, Twann Johnson, Reeda Johnson.

Arkansas: Alexander Collins, Caleb Lorren, Jason Daniel Lorren, Stephanie Lorren, Lakisha Keys, Patrick Jerome Pettus, Jr., Juain Young, Jamey Martin, Mark & Amanda Haughn, Arisha Johnson, William Clay Stover, Kofi Adzokpa, Renarda & Helen Williams, Elvis & Tanya Easterwood, Steve Alison, Paula Bell, Marty Haughn, Leonard Burgest, Zenobia Harley, Patricia Ward, Debra Cumberbatch, Darryl Walker, Kevyn Wayne, Chris Rhodes, Louise Yahon, Shawnise Powell, Alexis Powell, Marcia Shelton, Lori Ducy, Shelly Sutherland, Phyllis Moragne, Ellen Brown, Dustin Nwoling, Sue Harris Henderson, Aeriel Wright, Theresa Carter, Kreth Simmons, Emmory Simmons.

Texas: Briana J. Miller, Derrick Johnson, Haile Yosabe, Megan

Giles, Israel Bladimir Munoz, Sonia Munoz, Robert Lee Contreras, Gina Contreras, Rene Rodarte, David Rodarte, Angela Austin, Africa Stinson, Eleza Ambaiy, Ricard Boakye, Cynthia Opoku.

Virginia: Aicha Fadiga, William Sano (Morris), Xavier Sano, Kiara Tibbs, Jeanet Williams, Calvin Gillard.

France: All friends and family members.

Ivory Coast: Lancine Allassane Sanon and all friends and family members.

California: Karen and Ronnie Frost.

Florida: Namassa Sanogo, Mohamed Sylla, Aicha Sylla.

Oume: All my family members from the Toure and Sanon compounds.

Gabon: Kassoum Sanogo, Ibrahima Traore, Yacouba Sanogo, Keleti Traore, Sangone Safi.

Indiana: Bobby Reagor and Diaka Burruss.

PART I

Diaka

Chapter 1

⌒∞⌒

Things were strange in the compound when Mama was sick. Which seemed to be more often lately. Usually when Diaka came rushing home from school, she'd meet her mother in the communal kitchen shared by the women that lived in their fourteen-unit compound. On most days, Diaka dropped her schoolbooks at her family's small, three-bedroom unit, changed out of her school uniform and rushed to the kitchen to help her mother.

It was always fun being there with her mum and the other women, all speaking their different dialects from their various tribes, but somehow understanding each other because they all spoke French, and the main dialect, Mandingo. As they turned fufu in big metal pots over the three-stone fire, or fried *alloko*, they chatted loud and fast about everything—children, their husbands, the price of food in the market, and private women things they always said in code when their young daughters were with them.

Today, Diaka dropped her books in her room and lingered for a few moments before heading toward her parents' bedroom across the small hallway. Like most houses in the area, theirs was a wood-frame, plywood house with cement floors and an aluminum roof. It was crowded with furniture and knick-knacks her father collected while out on the streets of Abidjan working.

She heard her parents' door open and then close and then heard a fiercely whispered argument between her father and her Aunt Namassa, her mother's only sister.

"You have to take her to the hospital. It's worse than it has been," Aunty Namassa said. Mama had been having stomach problems for the last year. Usually the concoctions from the herbalist would clear the pain and running stomach, but for the past few days, they weren't helping.

From the long pause from her father, Diaka knew he was stroking his chin and measuring his words before he spoke. She held her breath. With the way Mama had been looking, she hoped and prayed her father would take her to the hospital.

Diaka knew his answer before he spoke it. "There's no money for the hospital. The herbalist knows what he's doing. He just gave some new medicines and is sure she'll be fine in the next few days."

"Let me take her then." Diaka could hear her aunt trying to control the level of her whisper. She didn't know if it was because she didn't want Mama to hear or because she knew Papa's stubbornness and temper and that it was better to persuade him gently, if at all.

"I can take care of my family."

"Moussa..." Diaka heard Aunty Namassa let out a deep breath. "Where are the herbs then? Let me go and boil them."

Diaka heard paper rustling and then her father said, "She has to drink everything for it to work. Boil it for ten minutes and then give it immediately."

The sound of her father's keys rang through the hallway, and then the front door slammed. Her father was a dollar van driver and usually picked customers from the time they left for school in the morning until late when it was time to eat dinner. He had been working less and less to stay and take care of Mama when Aunty Namassa couldn't come. She had a husband of her own to look after.

Diaka waited a few minutes and then walked out to meet her aunt in the small corridor. She stood there frowning, holding a brown paper bag.

"Diaka, you've come?"

"Yes, Aunty." She ran into her aunt's arms for a quick embrace.

"How was school?" Her aunt patted her on the head and smoothed her hair back.

"Good, Aunty." Diaka fell in step with her aunt, hoping to follow her to the kitchen. "Are you going to cook?"

"Yes, but you know you'll be staying here to do your schoolwork. Your education is important."

Diaka frowned. Her mother always let her stay in the kitchen for half an hour, chatting and cooking with the other women. At twelve years old, she could cook pretty much any dish, but only got to cook a dish from start to finish on the weekends and during the holidays when there was no school. Even though they weren't educated themselves, her parents stressed the importance of Diaka and her eight-year-old twin brothers getting an education so their lives could be different. Better.

"Did you greet your mother?"

Diaka shook her head and looked down at her shoes her aunt had found in the market for her. The cobbler had just fixed the soles and she hoped they would last for the rest of the school year.

Her aunt pushed her towards her parents' room. "Go and greet your mother, child. She will be fine. Then change out of your school uniform and start your homework." Her voice was firmer than usual. Diaka knew she was worried about her sister. She said she would be fine, but would she?

Diaka's legs trembled a little as she padded toward her parents' room. She hated seeing her mother sick and in pain. Her mother usually worked hard, preparing them for school in the mornings, then did laundry by hand, cleaned the house, swept their part of the compound, sometimes went to the market, cooked, and then joined the family for their evening meal. Her face was always shining. She sang all day, as if the work made her happy.

She was a good mother. She didn't scream and shout or beat them like the other mothers in the compound. When she told them to do something, Diaka and the oldest of the twins, Baba obeyed immediately. The youngest twin, Morris, was a bit naughty and sometimes had to be persuaded with a firm look or a raised voice. But theirs was a peaceful household where her parents loved each other, and the children respected their parents.

When Diaka heard her mother call out for her aunt, she forgot all about her fears and rushed to her mother's side. "Mama, what is it?"

Her mother smiled a weak smile and pulled her close. "Diaka, you're home. My good girl. How was your day?"

"It was good, Mama. Do you need some water? Should I bring you some soursop?" The fruit seemed to be the only thing that calmed Mama's stomach.

"No, my dear. Just sit here for a few minutes."

Mama's smile was weak. Her eyes weren't clear. Diaka buried her face in her mother's chest. She wished she could erase the last year of sickness–her mother growing smaller and paler, the house always smelling like the boiled herbs in the bitter drinks that were supposed to be making her well.

It was difficult having a stomach problem when living in a compound where fourteen units had to share the same bathroom. Aunty Namassa had bought a bucket to keep at Mama's bedside and it was Diaka's task to keep it clean. The smell rising from it let her know it was time to carry out that duty.

Her mother turned her head as she hurried out of the room with it. Diaka hurried past the row of shower stalls to the row of pit toilets and dumped the bucket. She cleaned it with Detol and rushed back into the house.

When she got back to her mother's bedside, her mother smoothed the back of her hand against her cheek. "My good, sweet girl."

She frowned and tried to straighten Diaka's hair. It had been two weeks since it had been braided, and it looked messy. Diaka hoped one of the women in the compound or maybe Aunty Namassa would braid it for her soon. Mama was too sick to do it.

Diaka would give anything to feel the soft touch of her mother's hands on her scalp, putting oil before braiding. Her touch was even soft while braiding, unlike everyone else who felt like they were trying to pull her hair right off her head.

Mama took her time to sit up in the bed. Diaka helped pull her frail upper body up and then moved her pillows behind her to hold her up.

Mama's fingers trembled as she held on to Diaka's arms. She lifted a thin arm and pointed to her old suitcase in the corner. "Go and look inside my box and bring a small purse from the corner. It's brown."

Diaka dug in the suitcase for a while before she found an old, tattered wallet wrapped in a faded loincloth. She brought it to her mother's bed and sat beside her again. She wanted to tell her to lie down and rest and wanted Aunty Namassa to hurry and come with the new herbal concoction that would make her better.

Her mother's small fingers pushed around in the wallet until she finally smiled. She pulled out a chain with a square shaped, golden trinket at the end. She pulled Diaka close and placed it in her hand. The gold had a deep shine to it that made Diaka know it must cost a lot of money. She turned it over in her hands and brought it close to her eyes so she could see.

The square part of the necklace had the imprint of a bull on one side and a lion on the other side. She looked up at her mother for an explanation.

Her mother spoke, "I received this from my mother when I was your age. It's been passed down in our family for one hundred years. Always keep it safe and close to you. The lion will always give you courage and the bull will give you strength in the face of adversity."

She folded Diaka's hands closed over the necklace and wrapped her own hands around hers and squeezed. "When your first child is old enough, you give this and explain our family tradition. You hear me?"

Diaka nodded and pressed her face against her mother's chest. She and her mother had always been close, but she had never felt closer to her than in this moment.

When she finished, she lay back against the pillows and began singing she and Diaka's song.

Ohhh!! Life...from the time we are born,
We came from somewhere and at death we are going somewhere.
In between we will do all our best to love, guide, cherish those GOD gives us
With all the power He gives us.
Family should love and support one another without any conditions.
We are family, we are family,
We will stand and absorb the pain and gain of this life together.
We will forgive one another and forgive others as life goes on.
The current flowing thru all humanity is LOVE,
Let's LOVE, LOVE, LOVE ourselves,
Each other, anywhere we are.

They sang together for a while. Diaka loved the sound of her mother's voice, gliding over the melody she had sung for her since she was a baby. She wished she would sing the song forever, but she knew the singing was making her mother tired, so she wanted to make her stop. Just as she was about to hush her, Aunty Namassa's voice joined them from behind.

She sang strong and loud, almost as if she wanted to let Mama know she didn't have to sing. She'd do the singing for her. Mama closed her eyes and stopped singing and smiled while Aunty Namassa and Diaka finished the song together.

Aunty Namassa brought over a steaming mug. "Diaka, you haven't changed your clothes. You should be doing your schoolwork."

Mama pulled Diaka into the bed with her. "Let her stay for a while. Her homework will wait."

Aunty Namassa pressed her lips together. She brought the cup to the bed, made her sister drink half of it, then set it on the table near the bed. Diaka thought at first Aunty was angry that she had disobeyed and not gone to do her schoolwork, but realized her eyes held only sadness.

She quietly left the room, probably to go back to the kitchen to cook dinner. Sometimes she came over to cook and other times, the other women in the compound cooked for them. Sometimes they brought their own food and other times, they took groceries from Diaka's family house to cook with. Everyone was working to feed their own families and even though they shared, they couldn't feed a whole family every day.

Diaka lay next to her mother, humming their song until she could feel her mother's breathing becoming deep. Just as her mother let out a light snore, she heard the front door slam. Her brothers were home. They were still in primary school and got out a little later than Diaka.

She heard their footsteps running toward their room to drop their books and she knew it would be seconds before they came tumbling and yelling into her parents' room. She gently pulled herself away from her mother and went to stop them before they could come in. She shut their parent's door and met them in the hallway.

"Where's Mama? I'm hungry."

"Mama is sleeping. Aunty Namassa will bring fried fish and *attieke* soon. Go and change your uniform."

Baba pointed to Diaka. "You're still wearing your uniform."

Diaka looked down as if she had forgotten. She pushed her brothers toward their room. "Go and change."

Morris darted around her arms. "I want to see Mama. Why is she sleeping? Is she sick again? I wish she would stop being sick. I like her food better than Aunty Namassa's. Let me help Mama out of bed so she can cook."

He started running toward their door, but Diaka grabbed him by the collar. "Leave her. She needs to sleep, wicked boy. Does every child have good food to eat?" She grabbed his ear and twisted it. "Go and change your clothes now before I tell Papa and you get a beating."

Morris sulked, but followed Baba to their room.

The rest of the afternoon passed quickly. Diaka breezed through her homework as she always did. School came easy to her. Her parents often talked of her going to university and whether she would become an accountant or go into nursing and maybe even medical school. They smiled at her with pride in their eyes and said she was the hope of their family. She would succeed and lead the family out of poverty.

She had to leave her room a couple of times to break up fights between her brothers while they were trying to do their homework. They didn't love school like Diaka and did their work more to avoid their father's cane than wanting to learn.

Their father came home a few hours later. The boys ran out to greet him, followed by Diaka. He rubbed their heads and their bellies but didn't ask them about their school day or how they were feeling. He didn't make the boys laugh by tickling their sides. There were lines in his forehead and his mouth was thin and tight as he gently pushed the boys behind him and went into his bedroom.

The boys followed. They hadn't been allowed to see their mother the whole afternoon because she was sleeping. They ran to her bedside and were both grabbed by their father's strong hands just as they were about to pounce on her.

"Be still. Your mother is resting." He held them until they calmed down.

"Jeneba, I've come home." The sound of their mother's name on their father's lips was always a sweet sound to Diaka. She wondered whether a man would say her name like that one day.

Mama roused from sleep with a smile on her face.

The lines disappeared from Papa's forehead. He sat on the side of the bed and grasped Mama's hand. "Did you drink all your medicine?"

She nodded. She looked past him. "Are those my boys? I've been waiting for you."

Baba and Morris looked at Papa to make sure it was okay and then climbed into the bed on either side of their mother. She asked them questions about school and their day. She gave Morris a pinch for being naughty in school, but instantly smoothed the place where she had pinched him with those soft hands of hers.

Normally, Baba and Morris would run around shouting and playing with the other kids in the compound after finishing their schoolwork until they had to be forced to come in for dinner. Diaka had friends in the compound that she played with as well, but today, they all stayed gathered in her parents' room. They even ate dinner with Mama on the bed.

Everyone talked and laughed and told stories as if it was a normal thing. Diaka felt better after the meal. Mama seemed better. She was stronger when talking and her eyes shone like they hadn't in a long time. She told story after story about her childhood and how she met Papa and how he won her heart. And then how Diaka and then the twins were born and how her heart grew a little bigger the first time she saw each of their faces.

Maybe the herbalist was right. Maybe the new medicine was exactly what she needed. From the way things were looking, Mama would be back to normal in the next few days.

After they finished dinner, Papa put them to bed. Usually, he and Mama did it together. He said all the prayers and tucked them in. When he went back to his room, Diaka was surprised to hear music.

Mama loved to dance and most nights of the week, after the children went to bed, soft music trickled out of her parents' bedroom door. Diaka loved to sneak to her secret place where she could see and not be seen. Papa would hold Mama close, and they danced together. Papa was a terrible singer, but Mama didn't seem to mind. She only blushed when he sang the songs and kissed her cheeks while they danced.

Afterwards, Papa sat on his chair by the bed and rubbed Mama's feet while he told her crazy stories of the dollar van customers he had picked up that day. There was always an interesting story and sometimes an angry one, but mostly funny ones. Diaka loved to hear her parents laughing quietly about his customers from the day.

The music kept playing and Diaka snuck to her place outside her parents' room. She saw her father gently lift Mama out of bed. He held her as they danced, her feet not touching the floor. He carried her the whole time. Papa wasn't a tall man, only a little taller than Mama, but he was strong and muscular, so he danced her around the room with ease.

Diaka's heart burst at the smile on her mother's face. She heard them whisper, "I love you" to each other. Their love was strong. Perhaps Papa's love would be the strongest medicine, exactly what was needed to make Mama well.

Diaka settled into her bed, hoping and praying with all her heart that when she woke up, everything would be normal in their household again.

Chapter 2

Diaka's eyes popped open that next morning. It was Saturday and even though she didn't have school. She had to get up and help with the house chores. Diaka had heard Aunty Namassa come back late the night before. She had gone home to feed and spend some time with her husband, Solo, and her two children, and then came back to sleep in the parlor, just in case Mama got sicker during the night.

With the way Mama had looked dancing with Papa, Diaka was sure her mother was better. But Aunty Namassa still needed to be there to help with the Saturday house chores. She and Diaka would wash clothes, sweep and mop all the floors, go to the market and cook meals for Saturday and Sunday.

This would all be done dodging her brothers as they played all day. It seemed like they always wanted to play exactly where she was working. No matter how much she shouted at them, they were still underfoot. She smiled thinking about it. They got on her nerves, but she loved them.

Diaka got up and put on a t-shirt. It was full of holes but would be fine for the day's work. She tied a faded, frayed loincloth around herself. Aunty Namassa woke up with the sun, so it would be time to work soon.

Before Diaka could put on her flip-flops, she heard a loud wail coming from the direction of her parents' room. Her heart froze in her chest. It was Aunty Namassa. That kind of loud, heart-wrenching wail could only mean one thing.

Every part of Diaka's body shook as she ran from her room across the hall to her parents' room. Aunty Namassa was standing right in the doorway wailing her mother's name. "Jeneba, oh Jeneba. Why have you left me? Why have you gone to join our mother? You've left your children like your mother left us. Jeneba, oh Jeneba." It was a horrible, deep wailing song.

Diaka looked from her aunt to the bed. Why was Aunty Namassa crying? Mummy was there in the bed. Daddy was holding her and rocking her. Diaka started to run toward the bed to tell her mother to make Aunty Namassa stop singing that horrible song, but Aunty Namassa grabbed her.

Baba and Morris ran in the room. Their feet froze in the doorway right behind Diaka and their wailing aunt. Their eyes widened as they looked at their father cradling their mother and sobbing. Diaka wanted to ask them all what the problem was. Mummy was there in Papa's arms, right where she was supposed to be.

But then Diaka took a closer look at her mother. Her skin was a pale, ashen gray. Her eyes were open and had no light in them. They were just staring at nothing. Her mouth hung open wide, like she couldn't control it.

"Papa?" Diaka croaked to her father.

He looked up from his wife to Diaka and the look on his face answered her question. "Your mother is dead, Diaka. My Jeneba is dead."

Diaka screamed and took off running. Out the front door, through the compound and out the gate. She screamed the whole way. She was halfway up the busy, crowded street when she felt strong hands grabbing her arms. She was jerked backwards.

"Diaka, stop!" Aunty Namassa held her tight to keep her from running again. "Diaka!"

Diaka fell onto the dirty ground and began praying. She cried to God to not let her mother be dead. To wake up her mother in her father's arms. To make this whole terrible thing go away and everything be normal again. She screamed and cried and prayed, but there was no answer. Only people walking by, staring.

Aunty Namassa pulled her into her arms. "Diaka, my child. Come. Let's go home. I'm here. We're going to be fine. I'm going to take care of you. Come, child."

She kept speaking soothing words into Diaka's ear until Diaka allowed herself to be picked up off the ground and slowly carried back to the compound. By this time, many of the women in the compound had gathered and were wailing in the house and in the yard outside the house.

Hearing the chorus of cries, Diaka knew the unbelievable was true. Her mother was gone.

⚬⚬⚬

The next few months were a blur for Diaka. With her mother gone, she took on most of the household responsibilities. Aunty Namassa was able to help less and less, so Diaka had to do most of the cleaning, cooking, laundry and caring for her brothers. The other women in the compound helped shop at the market for her family, and sometimes they helped to cook, but most of the weight fell on Diaka.She did all this and had to continue at school. She felt tired most of the time but was determined to help her family.

Her brothers had become rascals at home and at school. They were in trouble daily with their teachers and with Diaka. Her father, in some ways, seemed to die with their mother. He sat around the house staring at the walls most of the time. He got really sick after her mum passed and could hardly work. He spent most of his days sitting in the chair next to his bed, staring at the place where his Jeneba used to lie.

Diaka could hear him crying late at night. She could tell he was trying to be quiet, but the sound of her father's weeping, muffled by a pillow, made her stomach ache. It made her afraid of bad things happening. When her father was sick, she wondered if she would lose him, too.

Diaka had her own nights of crying. She missed her mother. Missed how her mother took care of her when she was sick. How they cooked and cleaned together. She remembered the soft touch of her mother's hands on her scalp when she was getting her hair done. She would do anything to feel those hands again.

Aunty Namassa came by to help and to check on Diaka as much as she could, but she had increased her business so she could bring money and rice and other things for the family to eat. Diaka heard her aunt pleading with her father to shake himself and get back to work so he could take care of his family, but the next day, Diaka found him sitting in the chair by his bed, crying into one of her mother's dresses.

One day after school, Aunty Namassa showed up and joined Diaka in the kitchen. She was cooking groundnut stew. Her aunt fell in step beside her, chopping garlic and grinding other spices.

They worked in silence for a while until Diaka finally got the courage to ask what she had been thinking about for many days. "Aunty, you're very good at business, yes?"

"Yes, dear. A woman has to find something for her hands to do to help support her family."

"Yes, Aunty, it's true. I was wondering if you could help me to start a business. So I can be like you. So I can help my family."

"Hush, child. You're young. You're already doing too much with everything you're doing around the house. And school. You're twelve years old–still a child."

"Yes, but Aunty..." Diaka picked up another piece of garlic to peel. "You know Papa's not well, and the boys can't even focus in school because we don't always have food. You help us so much but...well... I want to do a business to help, too."

Aunty Namassa frowned as she fanned the flames to make the fire hotter. "What kind of business?"

Diaka smiled. She knew her aunt well enough to know she would at least consider her proposal. "Just a small fruit business.

I'll sell fruit on the street outside the compound. I'll only be sitting there so I can take my books outside with me and study until a customer comes. The boys can play outside near my stand so I can keep an eye on them. I'll only be out there a few hours every day, after I cook, and I'll be doing my homework. Please Aunty, you'll think about it?"

Aunty Namassa frowned again. "You're too young for everything that's happening in your life. You should be a child, thinking child thoughts, playing child games. Not worrying about how to care for your family."

Diaka shrugged. "My childhood died with my mother." She finished chopping the garlic and pushed it aside.

Aunty Namassa let out a deep breath. "I'll talk to your father about it."

Two weeks later, with money Aunty Namassa loaned her, Diaka opened her fruit stand on the street a little ways down from the compound. Their neighborhood was a cluster of compounds. Each compound was a string of small apartments joined together as one unit. Between the compounds there were busy streets with hawkers, provision stores, crowds of people, hustling to make a living. Diaka's fruit stand was right next to a provision store, so she picked up a lot of their business.

Diaka kept her promise to her aunt. She set up her fruit stand after she finished cooking meals for the next day. She sat at her stand with her books and lifted her eyes from the pages only when a customer approached. Her brothers played football on the street not too far from her stand.

That's how life went for the next few years. Diaka took care of her home and her father and brothers. Her fruit stand was successful enough that she could pay back the loan her aunt gave her and have money to help the household. She always gave the money to her father, so he wouldn't feel bad for not taking care of the family. He worked sporadically when his health allowed.

Diaka did better and better in school and when it came time for her to graduate from high school, she was among the top in her class. The whole compound was proud of her and the other mothers always told their children they needed to study hard and be like Diaka. Diaka would surely do something with her life and would be able to help her family even more.

The whole compound celebrated when Diaka graduated high school and was accepted to go to University of Abidjan. She was the first of her whole family to graduate high school and go to college. Her father's eyes seemed brighter those days. Except for when he mentioned how he wished his Jeneba were there to be proud of their daughter with him. She was doing and becoming everything they had dreamed for their children together.

Tears still came to his eyes if he looked at Diaka too long because she looked just like her mother. He would stare at her, then shake his head and look away, wiping a tear or two. Diaka knew her father, Moussa, would probably never marry again. Her mother was the love of his life and there was no room in his heart for another woman.

Diaka majored in business management at University of Abidjan. Business had saved her family and she wanted to know more and to do more. She and Aunty Namassa gathered enough money to pay just enough tuition for her to begin school. Then one day with a twinkle in her eye, Aunty Namassa said to Diaka, "Come, let me take you somewhere. I'll show you how you're going to finish paying for college."

She took her to the big market in the middle of town and showed her how to buy women's fashion including clothes, shoes, and jewelry. "You'll sell these at your school to the girls with money. You can make up to 50% profit. Even 75%."

That's exactly what Diaka did. She became known on campus as the girl with the styles. Anyone who had money, and even some that didn't, came to Diaka to supply them with clothing and shoes. For some, Diaka would let them pay half down and then pay the rest two or three weeks later. Her business grew, and she was able to pay for all four years of college and continue to support her family.

She was even able to buy a television for her family's apartment. There was only one other family in the compound with a television. Diaka, her brothers and all the neighborhood children used to gather outside Mr. Ali's window to watch television some evenings. Every once in a while, on the weekends, he would invite the children inside and they managed to behave and sit quietly, mesmerized by the pictures on the television screen.

Now her house was the one with the television. Her father was so proud of everything Diaka was able to accomplish. Since her mother died, sadness seemed to creep into her father's spine and he was always hunched over, with a frown on his face and worry lines in his forehead. But when Diaka graduated from college with honors and got a big job as an executive assistant in a finance company, his back straightened. He even smiled every once in a while.

Diaka had made her mother's dream come true. She had graduated high school and college and now had a job that would help her support the family. Aunty Namassa and her husband no longer had to take care of them, and Diaka enjoyed showering her aunt with surprise gifts for everything she had done for them over the years.

Even though things were hard, Diaka was determined to continue to make a better life for herself and her family.

Chapter 3

Diaka, thanks so much for getting this report to me so quickly. I appreciate your hard work."

Diaka nodded her acknowledgment to her boss and looked back down at the papers on her desk. Koffi Nguessan, the general manager of the company she worked for and her direct boss, stood in the door smiling at her. He did that often. Came to her office to ask for things instead of picking up the phone. Stayed longer than the conversation called for. Praised her more than necessary for every little bit of work she did.

He was a very handsome man—tall, dark and strong. He made Diaka nervous, but not in a bad way. When he smiled or said kind words to her, it made her stomach feel funny. Jumpy and anxious, like she was hungry or something.

He stood in the door with that dashing smile on his face. "Diaka, you're always working so hard. Have you eaten today?"

Diaka frowned and shook her head.

"Come with me. Let's go get something to eat."

Diaka's eyes flew open. She shook her head quickly.

Koffi laughed. "Well, you have to eat. What's the problem? It's not like I asked you to marry me or something. I just asked you to join me for lunch."

Diaka could feel herself blushing and was glad her skin was dark. She hoped he didn't notice. "I brought food with me. I need to stay and finish the other reports we discussed at the meeting."

Koffi frowned. "I'm the boss. And if the boss says you can take time away from work to go to lunch, then you should go."

Diaka's hands trembled a little. His frowning smile made him so handsome. Why was this man so nice to her all the time? She hadn't noticed him being this nice to the other workers. Maybe it was because she was his assistant. Maybe he was just appreciating her work. Everyone in the office talked of how things worked so much smoother since she was there. Even though she was an assistant, she often spoke up at meetings to offer suggestions. People who had been at the company longer than she had always seemed surprised at her ideas. Some of them had been implemented and had brought change to the way the office ran.

Maybe that's why Mr. Nguessan was always hanging around. He appreciated what Diaka was bringing to the office.

"Oh...okay." Diaka felt a funny feeling in the pit of her stomach. Something in her wanted to say no, but the smile on his face wouldn't let her. "I'll meet you outside in a few minutes."

He nodded and gave her a look. It was a different look than the one he usually gave her. Diaka recognized the look because her aunt always warned her about it when they shopped in the market together and men approached her.

"Diaka, you have to ignore these men. You know you're a beautiful girl with curves that make men imagine things about you they shouldn't. I know you like looking stylish but be careful about showing off your shape too much." Then her eyes would become wistful. "You're beautiful just like your mother. How could any man resist you?"

When they were in the market together, her aunt would hiss and send the men and their lusty eyes running. What would Aunty Namassa do if she could see the way Mr. Nguessan was looking at her now?

Mr. Nguessan took her to a restaurant fancier than she had ever been to before. When she saw the prices, she couldn't imagine why chicken should cost so much. Wasn't it just fried chicken and *attieke* like she prepared at home?

But he encouraged her to eat and eat well. So she drank soda and ate and enjoyed herself, trying not to focus on how much money was being wasted on a simple meal. People with money lived a different life.

He was very talkative and kept asking her questions. At first, she was very careful with her words. She didn't want to say the wrong thing to the boss. But he was so nice and kept complimenting her on everything from her work to her dress to her style and her voice. The more he complimented, the sweeter she felt inside. And the more he asked questions, the more she opened up and started talking to him.

She decided that he was just a nice person and wanted to treat her well for the way she behaved at work. He was a perfect gentleman through their whole lunch and took her back to the office in his nice car. Diaka had never ridden in such a nice car before.

That first lunch led to many others. Then dinners. And movies. Then trips to the beach on Saturdays. And expensive gifts – watches, jewelry, beautiful shoes and scarves.

Koffi introduced her to a life she didn't know existed in Abidjan. Her life was so much better since she had started working. She had rented the family a four-bedroom house and had it furnished with brand new furniture. With financial help from Koffi, she bought good groceries at the market and made sure her father and brothers ate well every day. Her father never went to work anymore since Diaka was making good money.

Her brothers hadn't finished high school. Both learned a trade, but they didn't have consistent work, so Diaka was the primary provider for the whole family. She felt proud that she could work hard and make sure they lived well.

But this life with Koffi was the next level. Nice cars with leather seats. Nice restaurants whose food tasted better than what she could prepare at home. It wasn't just survival or a notch above survival. It was extravagant and full of guilty pleasure. And she loved it.

And it wasn't just living a better life and enjoying fun that she couldn't afford on her own. Compliments about her work turned into compliments about her beauty and her body. Before she knew it, Diaka found herself always wanting to be with Koffi. She felt happiest when she was in his arms, looking at his face, and hearing his voice.

He brought a joy into her life that had died long ago when her mother died. She began to dream about the day when Koffi would ask her father to marry her. She dreamed of their traditional wedding and their church wedding. She dreamed of the children they would have.

She assumed she wouldn't be able to work at their company anymore when they got married. Maybe Koffi would let her stay home with their children. Or maybe he would support her to start her own business.

Diaka went to bed every night dreaming about her future life with Koffi, in their nice house, with their children and her getting her own car to drive and eating in restaurants. Maybe she would even get to travel out of the country one day.

God was rewarding her for the way she had taken care of her father and brothers. Now God was sending someone to take care of her.

Diaka was looking for the perfect time to introduce Koffi to her father. Every time she mentioned it though, his face got a funny look, and he started talking of how busy he was. As his assistant, Diaka knew he wasn't as busy as he said he was. Maybe he was looking for the perfect time, too.

Aunty Namassa had met him several times when she came to visit Diaka at the office. She agreed that he was handsome, but she said there was something about his eyes she didn't like. But she was happy that he was giving Diaka money to help with the family. And sometimes when he gave Diaka gifts, Diaka gave them to her aunt. So even though she was cautious, Aunt Namassa allowed the relationship with Koffi. She did keep saying that it was important that Diaka introduce him to her father. It wasn't proper for a girl to be dating a man without her father's blessing.

One day, Koffi asked to take Diaka away for the weekend. He showed her a beautiful brochure of a resort that took her breath away. Looking at the beautiful people on the cover, Diaka knew she had to go. She would have to go to the market to find a bathing suit and some beach clothes.

But she couldn't go away for the weekend with a man. They weren't married. Her father didn't even know about Koffi. What would she tell him?

But maybe this was the time Koffi planned to state his intentions to marry her. "This weekend will be a very special one for us, my dear."

What else could it be but the proposal she had been waiting on for months?

She told her father and Aunty Namassa she had to go for a training for work and went. There was no proposal, and Diaka felt like a fool. She wanted to tell Koffi that she never wanted to see him again, but she had gotten used to the fancy lifestyle and extra money to take care of her family. But she stayed angry with him for a week.

After five days of the silent treatment, he appeared at her desk with keys to a small used car. "It isn't much, but you can get around the city with it."

As he was teaching her to drive, squeezing her leg and caressing her arm the whole time, she forgave him. She had a car. She wondered if anyone in her whole family had ever owned a car.

So the next time Koffi asked her to go to the beach, Diaka lied to her father and went again. She told him she was spending the weekend at Aunty Namassa's house. Aunty Namassa agreed to cover her if she brought her back a nice gift.

The beach was so beautiful and the resort so lavish that Diaka pushed out of her mind the fact that she shouldn't be on vacation with a man she wasn't married to. She enjoyed feeling rich and carefree. She was having the time of her life.

Until she started feeling tired. And sick and drained. After it went on for weeks, she told Aunty Namassa about it.

Aunty Namassa sucked her teeth. "Don't tell me you've let that man get you pregnant." She insisted Diaka go to the clinic.

Diaka shuddered inside. Could that even be possible? Of course it could. She kicked herself. She had been pretending to be a rich, married woman at the beach without thinking of what she was actually doing. She could only blame the vomiting on eating bad fish one time. And since she had hired a girl to help out at home, she couldn't blame the tiredness on working at the office and at home.

The day after she talked to Aunty Namassa, Diaka went to a clinic that didn't require an appointment. The doctor listened to her for only a few minutes before telling her, "You're pregnant. Let's do the test. The results will be back tomorrow."

Diaka shook the whole time she was giving the sample for the test. Pregnant without being married? Well, surely this is what would make Koffi finally propose to her. He would be excited and finally make her his wife.

It was the longest night of her life–waiting for the next day when she would go get her test results. She stayed in her room without eating and barely answered her father when he came in to talk to her. The next day at the office, before she went back to the clinic, she was sullen and quiet.

She didn't laugh at any of Koffi's jokes and barely listened when he was talking to her about his plans for their weekend.

She wasn't sure how she got herself back to that doctor's office. When the doctor said, "You're pregnant," she nearly fell off the chair.

She started crying and wailing, not caring who could hear. The doctor kept trying to tell her that a baby was a blessing, but all she could think of was the look on her father's face when she told him she was pregnant. Hopefully, she would be able to tell him with Koffi at her side and a ring on her finger.

Diaka left the clinic and didn't even think of going back to work. She went straight to Aunty Namassa's house, hoping she'd be home from the market. When her aunt greeted her at the door, she fell into her arms weeping. Somehow her aunt led her into the parlor and sat her down on the couch, rocking her and comforting her. They hardly exchanged any words. Diaka cried and Aunty Namassa patted her on the back until she fell asleep in her arms.

She slept at Aunty Namassa's house that night. The next morning, she dressed in some clothes that she always left at Aunty Namassa's house. She took extra care to look beautiful. This would surely be the day Koffi proposed to her, after she told him the news. Her stomach was so upset, she couldn't eat breakfast. She hurried out of the house to get to work on time.

She sat in her office, waiting for Koffi's usual morning visit. He came to check on her every morning. Sometimes he would look around to see if anyone was in the corridor, then would close her door so he could steal a kiss or a caress.

She was feeling so bad, she couldn't even muster a smile to greet him when he came.

He frowned when he saw her face. "Why are you looking so sad? What's been wrong with you, Diaka? With all I do to make you happy, why is your face looking sad and tired all the time lately?"

Diaka shook her head. He was right. Koffi worked hard to make her happy. What was she so upset? She was pregnant with this man's baby and all he wanted was her happiness. He had shown her that in the eight months they'd been together.

She looked up at him. "I need to tell you something." She cleared her throat. "Something important...and private."

Koffi looked down the corridor and then closed her door. "What is wrong, my darling? What's keeping you from enjoying the happiness I bring you?"

Diaka felt better hearing the sweetness in his voice. She motioned for him to pull the chair in the corner closer to her desk.

She waited until he was sitting and then took a deep breath. "I went to the doctor today. I'm pregnant." She forced a small smile. "We're having a baby."

Koffi's smiled faded so quickly, it looked like he had a different face. "Pregnant? We?"

Diaka nodded. The pit of her stomach started to turn.

Koffi stood up so fast, the chair fell. "It's not my child. It can't be my child. You can't put another man's child on me. How could you say that?"

Diaka's face filled with horror. "Another man? There is no other man. You're the only man I spend my time with. You're the only man I've ever been with. This is your child."

Koffi leaned across her desk and whispered loud and fierce, right in her face. "You're not going to put this child off on me. Now listen to me clearly, let this be the last time I hear you say anything about this being my child. You can keep your job, but you can't tell anyone anything about this. You need to go to whatever man you've been sleeping with and tell him about his child. But don't try to put this on me."

Diaka sat there with her mouth open. She couldn't find words, let alone speak. But she had to say something. Had to convince him that was his baby. That he needed to come see her father and ask to marry her. "I...you...we..." she burst into tears, rocking back and forth. "Why, Koffi, why?"

Koffi paced back and forth in her small office space. He stopped and pointed a long finger at her. "Go home and get yourself together. Decide what you're going to do. Like I said, you can keep your job as long as you never speak of this again. Don't tell anyone you thought this was my child. You hear?" He scowled at her and jerked her door open and stormed out.

Diaka was left at her desk in complete shock. How could he think she had been with another man? She spent every extra moment with him. Did he not remember their weekends at the beach and Sunday afternoons at his house? When could she have time for another man? Did he think she was the kind of woman that slept with many men? Didn't he know how much she loved him and was waiting to become his wife?

She gathered herself up and stumbled out of the building to

her car. When she got there, the tears started flowing. How could Koffi say those things to her? Think those things about her? What was she going to do now? She couldn't go to her father's house without Koffi and a ring. What could she tell him? This kind of disgrace on their family would surely kill him.

Straining to see through a constant stream of tears, Diaka drove to Aunty Namassa's house. When she told her aunt everything that happened, she was in shock. Tears began to pour down Aunty Namassa's face. Which made Diaka cry harder. Her aunt wiped her face and told Diaka not to worry. She would figure out what to do.

Her aunt sat there for a while thinking. Diaka wished she would talk out loud. The silence was making her even more afraid.

She finally said, "Don't worry, Diaka. I'll go to his office tomorrow and talk to him. He was shocked, but after he's had time to think about it, he'll change his mind. He'll go see your father."

Diaka nodded, tears streaming down her face the whole time. She hoped her aunt was right. Otherwise, what would she do?

Chapter 4

Diaka slept at Aunty Namassa's house again that night. If you could call it sleep. She was awake the whole night, reliving every moment of her time with Koffi. Every wonderful romantic scene ended with the scene in her office with him walking away from her. How could he do that? How could he think that about her?

Aunty Namassa hurried off to see him the next morning. Diaka waited at the house for her call. She knew her aunt would take care of everything like she always did. Soon, they would all be standing in front of her father together.

But two hours later, a child from down the street knocked on the door. "There's a call for you." Anxious to hear how her aunt had fared, Diaka rushed down the street to the neighborhood phone.

"My dear Diaka..." the tone of her voice said everything. "He's refused you and he's refused his child. There was another secretary sitting at your desk. Come down here and we'll face him together."

Diaka's hands shook the whole time she was driving to the office. She arrived about thirty minutes later and found her aunt exhausted and tired sitting on a bench outside her office building. When Diaka saw the distress on her face, she burst into tears again.

Aunty Namassa pulled her down onto the bench. "Diaka, pull yourself together so you can confront him. Stop crying and stand like a woman. We need him to know he can't get away with this. If he's not going to marry you, he will still have to take care of this child. And he can't fire you from your job. Who is his boss? We may have to talk to his superiors to handle this situation."

Diaka wrung her hands, wishing the whole situation would just go away. She and her aunt went up the four flights of stairs and sat at the receptionist area, waiting for him to come out. Diaka wondered what he had told the receptionist. The young woman was normally very friendly with Diaka, but now she kept looking at her like she was a dirty rag on the floor.

About an hour later, Koffi came out of his office. As soon as he saw them, he started yelling. "Did you misunderstand me?"

He looked frantically between Diaka and Aunty Namassa. "You foolish women are trying to force a child on me that's not mine. Is that how you plan to make it in this world? Trying to force a man to marry you to rescue you from your poverty?" The look he gave Diaka filled her with shame. He had never called her poor before.

Filled with anger, she stood up, yelling almost as loud as him. "This is your child. I don't sleep around. You're the first and only man I've ever slept with. Ever. And my family might be poor, but we're a very honorable family. And as a believer of God, I could never sleep around with many men and then try to say it's yours. This is your child." She pointed to her still small, tight belly. The heat of her emotions caused her voice to rise. "Your child. Whether you want to believe it or not. In fact, we can take a test."

"I'm not taking any test. That's not my child!" He turned to his secretary. "Call security. Have them thrown out of here. And warn the security guards they should never return here again!"

He bent over and picked up a box next to the receptionist's desk. "Here are your things. Don't ever come here again." The snarl on his face made him look like a monster. Where was the charming smile, the sweet voice, the gentle hands she had known for those eight months?

He kicked the box, and it slid across the floor and stopped at

Diaka's feet. Diaka looked down at her belongings. Her whole life in this office was reduced to the size of a small box.

As Koffi stormed off, Aunty Namassa called out to his back, "God will deal with you. God will repay you for this." She cursed him loud enough for the whole office to hear.

As Diaka and Aunty Namassa were escorted out of the building by the stern security officer, Diaka was completely humiliated. She had been living in a dream with Koffi and now she was waking up. She wished she could go back to sleep and enjoy her dream again.

What would she do now? How could she tell her father? How could she continue to take care of her family without a job? How would she make sure her father and brothers continued to eat well every day, without a care for how the rent and bills would be paid? She had taken care of them for so many years. She would have to find a new job quickly. Or maybe start a new business. But how could she do that while pregnant?

Diaka cried, stumbling down the street, hugging her box to her chest. She got into her car and Aunty Namassa slid in beside her. She cried until all her tears were spent. Her aunt only sat there shaking her head. Her face looked so hopeless that it scared Diaka. "Aunty, what do I do now?"

Her aunt sat there for a second, biting her lip. "You'll let me tell my husband, your uncle, Solo, eh? He will come with us when we go meet your father."

Diaka nodded. Having him there to help break the news would hopefully ease the situation.

"You need to go home tonight. You've been at my house for two days now and you know he doesn't like it when you're away for too long. Tell him that me and Uncle Solo will be coming to meet him tomorrow."

Diaka nodded. She dropped Aunt Namassa at her house and dreaded the long ride home to hers.

Her father barely looked up from the television when she entered. That had become his life. Sitting and watching the television and eating the good food Diaka provided and their house help cooked. Diaka winced. With no job, she would have to let the house help go and they would have to eat cheaper meals until she could find another job.

"Papa, please, can I ask for something?"

Moussa looked away from the television. "Yes, my daughter. Anything. How could I refuse you, a wonderful daughter that's made her father proud?"

Diaka put on a strained smile. "Please, Aunty Namassa and Uncle Solo will be coming tomorrow evening to speak with you about something. Is that okay?"

"Of course. You'll have that girl prepare a nice meal to welcome our guests?"

Papa had gotten used to showing off whenever guests came over. They always served chicken, fish or beef.

"Of course, Papa." They should enjoy one last meal as a family together before Diaka began cutting their spending.

Diaka quietly performed her house duties and retreated to her bedroom. The next day, she went to her aunt's home and stayed there all day. She helped with the cooking and cleaning and other small tasks while her aunt was away at the market. Her family didn't know she had lost her job, so she had to stay away from home and pretend she was at work.

That evening when Aunt Namassa returned from the market, she set the table and dished food for her husband and children. When she was finished, she called Diaka and led her out to the backyard to sit under the shade tree to talk. They joined hands and Diaka began to cry before Aunt Namassa even said a word.

Her aunt cupped her face in her hands. "My Diaka, daughter of my sister Jeneba, I love you."

Diaka cried even harder.

"Your mother would be so proud of you. You are a good woman, just like she was. Ever since you were a young girl, looking at your face and watching your conduct was like looking at and watching my sister." She continued, "What you are about to face with your father is frightening and we don't know the outcome, but I want you to know that no matter what happens, I am right there with you and we will fight together just like me and your mother did when we lost our mother."

She lifted Diaka's chin. "Your mother was a strong woman. She taught you to be strong too, so you hold your head up and fight!"

Diaka placed her head on Aunt Namassa's shoulder. Her aunt began humming her sister's favorite song that she and Diaka sang together. She rubbed Diaka's hair and wiped her tears. It reminded Diaka of her mother rubbing her scalp when she was sick and singing their song. It made her feel a little better for the moment.

Diaka left her aunt's house in enough time to reach home at the usual time she would arrive from work. She stopped in the kitchen to see if dinner was almost ready, dreading the fact that she would have to fire her house help the very next day. The girl's life had changed a lot since she had been working for Diaka's family and now she would be broke again and unable to pay her school fees.

About an hour later, she heard a knock on the door and her heart rose to her throat. Aunty Namassa and Uncle Solo were there, and it was time to tell her father and brothers all her sad news.

Her father, Moussa, opened the door with a big smile. "Sister, brother, you have come. You are welcome to our home. Come in, please."

Diaka set the dinner plates on the table. She could tell from her father's laughter he was anxious to hear what Namassa and Solo needed to talk to him about.

When the whole family was seated around the table, they made idle chatter. Diaka knew it was only a matter of time. Her stomach was in knots. She couldn't eat the chicken on her plate.

When everyone had finished eating, Papa cleared his throat and addressed Uncle Solo. "You have come from a long distance. What news do you have for me today?"

Namassa and Solo look at each other. Uncle Solo spoke, "Brother, let's move into the living room so we can discuss things well."

Diaka winced when she saw the frown on her father's face. He knew what was coming wasn't good news. The whole family moved to the living room. Diaka sat on the edge of her seat, fingering her hair nervously.

Papa looked around and then spoke. "Solo, I do welcome you in my home with laughter, but it seems you need to tell me and my family some serious news. Please, do not hold back from telling us now."

Solo looked at his wife and then at Diaka. Papa looked at Diaka because he could tell that the news involved her. He said to Diaka, "My daughter, what is it that you know of this news?"

Diaka looked at her father and tried to speak. Her mouth was moving, but no words were coming out.

Uncle Solo rescued her. There was a loud humming sound in Diaka's ear so she could barely hear her uncle remind her father of how long they'd known each other, and how much he respected him and loved his family. He said that although something unusual had taken place, by God's blessing and his understanding, it could be solved and life could move forward.

Diaka held her breath as he explained about Diaka's relationship with Koffi and how she had been expecting marriage. He went on for long about how well Koffi had treated Diaka. "He loved her very much. Until the moment that Diaka told him that she's pregnant with his child. Then it became another story."

Papa nearly fell off his chair. Morris and Baba sat there with their mouths open. They all stared at Diaka, as if they had never seen her before.

Uncle Solo continued, "Unfortunately, this man, Koffi, was Diaka's boss. She has lost her job, and he refuses to accept the child or her.

Hearing her uncle's words, Diaka began sobbing in her chair.

Her brothers came to her and held her, kissing her cheeks gently without saying a word. Her father sat there speechless.

Uncle Solo looked at his wife, then at Diaka, then back to Papa. He finally spoke, "Moussa, I know you to be an understanding man and Diaka needs our care, especially because her former boss refuses to help. You know Diaka to be a smart, kind and good woman that you raised well. She did not do this intentionally. On behalf of Diaka, my wife and Jeneba, I ask that you, Baba and Morris understand what has happened and forgive Diaka for any humiliation and shame that may come upon the family, and accept your daughter with the unborn child without any more stress to her."

Aunty Namassa spoke for the first time since the meeting started. "Diaka will find work and continue to care for herself and you all. Everything will be fine."

Diaka's twin brothers nodded their heads softly in agreement as they held their sister close in their arms.

Papa finally spoke. "Solo, my daughter is pregnant without being married? Are you telling me the truth?"

Uncle Solo nodded.

Papa walked over to Diaka's chair and knelt down, pushing her brothers aside. He looked up at Diaka. "Daughter, are you pregnant?"

Tears fell from her eyes. "Yes, Father, I am."

Her father stood and walked away from her. "Namassa, Solo, this is not acceptable in my family. I will not tolerate her being pregnant by a man without being married to him. She has humiliated me. Everyone in our whole neighborhood who once looked up to Diaka will now speak of her indiscretions."

He looked back at Diaka and then turned back to them. "I don't want anything to do with her, the baby, or any of this situation. She is no longer welcome in this family."

Papa turned back to Diaka and the hateful look on his face was even worse than the one on Koffi's. "Pack your things and leave. This is no longer your home. I am no longer your father. Go!"

Aunty Namassa started crying. She, her husband and Diaka, knelt down at Papa's feet. "Please, Moussa. You can't take this kind of decision. Your family has been through too much. Please now."

Papa walked away from them. He turned just before going into the corridor. "She should be gone by the morning. My decision is final."

Diaka fell into a heap on the floor, crying uncontrollably. She heard her father call from his room. "In fact, Baba, Morris, come and pack your sister's things. Take them out to the door. She shouldn't spend another night in this house."

Her brothers looked at Diaka helplessly. Aunty Namassa made them sit while she went and packed Diaka's things.

That evening, Diaka left her family and her house and everything she had bought to make it a home for her father and brothers. The worst had happened. She couldn't even imagine what she would do next.

Chapter 5

Diaka heard a knock on the door of her bedroom at Aunty Namassa's house. It was a tiny storage room they had cleaned out and put a mattress on the floor for her to sleep.

Diaka couldn't ignore the second knock. "Yes?"

Her aunt opened the door. "Diaka, are you still sleeping? It's almost noon. I just came back from the market to check on you."

Diaka turned toward the wall and pulled the blanket over her head.

Her aunt sat on the mattress beside her and gently pulled the blanket down. "Diaka, have you even eaten today? And when was the last time you bathed? You have a child growing inside of you that needs to be fed. You have to take care of your body. You can't live like this."

Diaka burst into tears. "That's just it, Aunt Namassa. I don't want to live. I don't want to live anymore. Just leave me here and let me die and go join my mother."

Diaka sobbed into the mattress. She had been at Aunt Namassa's house for almost a month. She sat around the first few days almost in a trance, crying at how she had been living on top of the world and lost everything–her job, her man, her finances and her family. She had nothing. Nothing except a baby growing inside her that she wasn't even sure she could care for.

After realizing her predicament, she had begun helping Aunt Namassa around the house and in the market, but soon she began to realize that everyone knew about her. They knew she had foolishly gotten pregnant by a man that didn't want her and that she had been disowned by her father and thrown out of her own house. Small neighborhoods thrived on gossip, and by the time the stories came back around to Diaka, they were ten times worse.

Every time she heard the gossip about her, she wanted to die. She was a prostitute. That's how she could afford everything she had bought. God was punishing her for sleeping with a married man. One version of her story said she had AIDs and was spreading it around to any man that was foolish enough to sleep with her.

As the rumors about her grew, Diaka would no longer come out of the house. When she reflected on her situation, she reached the point where she didn't get out of bed anymore. She knew it wasn't good for her or the baby, but she didn't care. They would both be better off in heaven.

"Diaka, don't speak like that. Life is a gift. Your life and the baby's life. Do you want to add to my sorrow again by dying? Do you think my heart can take losing you, too?"

Diaka sniffled and sat up in the bed. She hadn't thought about how her dying would affect Aunt Namassa. She sat there for a second and then burst into tears again. "You'd be better off without me."

Aunt Namassa hissed and rubbed her hands together. "Mighty God, what am I to do with this child?" She paced around the tiny space, wringing her hands and calling out to God for answers. She finally sat down on the bed and began rubbing Diaka's head and humming Diaka and her mother's song.

Diaka cried harder, feeling her aunt's fingers on her scalp. She felt her mother's love in that moment and knew she couldn't break her aunt's heart by willing herself to die. "What can I do? What can I even do?"

Aunt Namassa continued humming. She stopped abruptly. "I think I have an idea." She waited until Diaka turned herself over on the mattress and looked at her. "Would you like to get away from here for a while? To go have the baby somewhere else and then come back and start over again?"

Diaka stared at the ceiling, thinking. "That would help. Being away from this city. The gossip. The memories..." She thought about being able to be away from everything and felt a little better. "But how would I care for myself? I have no money and no job."

"Don't worry about that. You would be well cared for. Let me check on something and I'll let you know. It could take up to a week."

Aunt Namassa jumped up off the mattress and started toward the door. "Diaka, I'm not asking you. Get up and bathe and come to the kitchen and eat while I work my plan."

Six days later, Aunt Namassa came running into the house, breathless. She met Diaka in the kitchen, frying *alloko*. She had been feeling better since she knew her aunt was working on a better life for her. Even though she had no idea what it was, at least she had some hope."Diaka, the answer has come. God has favored you. All will be well." Her aunt motioned for her to come sit at the dining table to hear her news.

Diaka washed her hands and rushed to the table. "What is it, Aunty?"

Aunt Namassa took a long sip of water from the glass Diaka brought her. It seemed like it took her forever to swallow and start talking. "My friend, Poupette, used to live here in Abidjan for many years. We were very close, almost like sisters. When she got married and had children, she decided to move back to her village, Oume. It's about 700 km from here."

Diaka nodded and frowned, wondering what all this had to do with her predicament.

"I wrote to Poupette and she and her husband have spoken to

the chief of the village and he's agreed they will hear you and hopefully allow you to come live there. The people will take good care of you and you can eat well and be healthy. The baby can be healthy, and you can birth your child in peace." Aunty Namassa spoke fast, waving her hands with excitement. "This is a blessing from God. At last, you will have peace."

Diaka took it all in. Her aunt had arranged for her to move to a village, far away from everything. It would be scary to be away from everything she knew, but then again, she had nothing here anymore. Maybe this was just what she needed. A fresh, new place where she could have her baby in peace. But what if the people there started gossiping about her, too?

Her aunt spoke as if she'd heard her thoughts. "People in the village love people from the city. They'll be so glad you're there. You will be well treated and well respected. Diaka, this is an answer from God. If you say yes, we'll leave in the next five days."

Diaka thought for a few more moments. What did she have to lose? "Okay, Aunty. I'll go to Oume."

Chapter 6

Diaka had never traveled out of Abidjan before. Her father often spoke of his village, but she had never been there. She had only heard the stories.

She packed all her clothes and started preparing to move far away from the only home she had ever known. She sold her car for a low price, just so she could get money for the move as quickly as possible. Village life would require candles, a lighter, a petroleum lamp, a heavy blanket for the cold, some soft shoes, a good flashlight with lots of batteries. She also wanted to pack some of her favorite candies and biscuits from the city.

On the day they were to travel, she and her aunt rose early to go to the car park. There weren't many vans to travel to Oume throughout the day and they wanted to be on the first one. The van was packed with people, five to a row that should seat four. The large woman next to Diaka was big enough to take up two seats. Diaka was glad she and Aunt Namassa were thin. There were bags and suitcases piled on top of the bus so high, Diaka wondered if the van would topple over if they took a sharp curve.

She realized she no longer wanted to die when the thought of dying in a van crash on the way to Oume began to worry her. When did she start wanting to live again? Maybe when the thought of starting over in Oume entered her heart. Or maybe that morning when she felt butterflies in her stomach and realized she had a life growing inside of her that she needed to be concerned about.

The feeling had shocked her. She had asked Aunt Namassa about it and she smiled and rubbed Diaka's small bulge of a stomach. "The child knows he's going home, and he's excited to be going there. Wonderful things will happen for this child there. I don't know what, but God will do wonderful things in this child's life in that village. You may think you're going to hide in shame, but God is working out something special just for this child."

Diaka nodded as hope began to grow like a small seed in her heart. Was God going to work everything out for her good? Could He fix the mess she had made of her life?

When the van finally filled with passengers, it was time to leave for Oume. As they passed the road leading to her old neighborhood, tears slid down Diaka's face. She hadn't gotten a chance to say goodbye to her brothers. Her father made it clear she wasn't welcome in his house and they weren't allowed to see her. She wondered how her father and brothers would maintain the house and continue to eat without her paying for everything. She whispered a small prayer for God to take care of them.

But she had herself and her child to take care of. How would she take care of herself in Oume? She guessed she would be living with her aunt's friend, Poupette, but was she supposed to eat and live there without paying any money? How would she afford the things she needed like toiletries and shoes when the ones she had wore out?

Whenever she asked Aunty Namassa these questions, she simply smiled and patted her arm and said that God and the people of the village would take care of her.

After they left Abidjan, the roads became rough and bumpy. The driver didn't have the sense to slow down. The van rattled, shook and jumped so hard that Diaka wondered if she would lose the baby before she even reached the village.

They had to stop at numerous police checkpoints and for bathroom breaks. They also slowed down to buy food from small vendors that ran alongside the van to sell their goods. The day seemed to stretch long. When they finally arrived at their destination, Diaka looked around. "This is Oume?"

Aunty Namassa shook her head. "No, we still have to walk about a mile."

Diaka frowned and looked at all her bags as they were being brought down from the top of the minivan. She was already tired and hot and now she had to carry her things for a mile walk on a dirt road?

Aunty Namassa smiled. "Don't worry, dear. We'll have plenty help."

Before they could gather their bags, two young boys that had been on the bus approached them. "Which village are you going to? Who are you going to visit?"

Diaka watched as her aunt told them where they were going and pointed to the bags. The boys picked them up and began walking down the stretch of road, beckoning for them to follow.

As they continued walking, children ran up to them. "Which family are you going to see?"

When Aunty Namassa gave her friend's name, the children smiled and clapped. One said, "We know exactly where Poupette lives. She lives on the other side of the tree, about a good thirty-minute walk from here." As they walked further down the road, they were surrounded by children, all following them and chattering the whole way. Diaka began to feel a strange feeling of home and comfort she couldn't explain.

After walking a long stretch, they reached the village around 6:30 p.m. The group of children and young people had grown to about forty and there was a large group of women waiting for them at the edge of the village. The children kept touching Diaka's clothes and admiring her shoes and asking her question after question about the city. Diaka was relieved when they finally arrived at Poupette's house after a long, tiring day of travel.

It was a mud house with a thatched roof. It was one of the largest houses they had passed in the village and had two bedrooms and a parlor with a door at the front and at the back of the house.

They sat in the main room, and Poupette brought them food to eat. About thirty minutes later, there was a knock on the door and then another and another—all women from the village bringing food and greetings.

Even though they were tired, Poupette and her husband Kaba thought it best that they see the chief before going to sleep. They sent a message to the chief and he sent a message back saying they were welcome.

Diaka was amazed at what she saw when she walked into the chief's palace. They were led into a large parlor with all sorts of wooden statues decorating the corners. There were large swatches of beautiful fabrics on the walls. The furniture seemed so fancy to be in this small village—intricately carved wood with beautiful silky fabric covering it. Everything looked rich and expensive.

As she was taking it all in, Poupette's husband, Kaba, stepped forward and addressed the chief. "Chief, may your blessing touch everyone in this village, for guiding us in the proper direction for years, and for saving lives as much as possible to improve our living conditions in this village. My wife and I have lived in our village for some time since we moved from the city years ago, and we feel great being home and also blessed to have a leader like you."

The chief nodded to acknowledge the pleasantries.

Kaba continued, "Today, we have an unusual circumstance that is confronting us, and we did advise you about it, and you accepted to hear us. We thank you for that. It is very much appreciated."

Kaba pointed towards her. "This is Diaka, the young woman who is in need of our help and you have accepted for her to live in our village with the condition that she provide you with the details of her circumstances so you can know how to assist her and make an announcement to the village requesting their help."

He turned and gestured toward Diaka. "Please speak to the chief now."

Diaka stood in front of the chief and his counsel. Her legs were trembling, and her hands were shaking. She clasped them together to hide her nervousness. Her voice shook as she began telling the chief and his counsel about her life. Her heart felt great sadness when she talked about her mother's death when she was twelve. She normally gleamed with pride when speaking of how well she did in high school and college and at her first job, but the shame from the rest of the story overshadowed any good feeling she may have had.

When Diaka told about her father kicking her out, she broke down and cried, so Aunty Namassa finished for her.

"Things were so overwhelming, she wanted to commit suicide. My husband and I tried everything we could to comfort her, but we realized that she needed to get away until her baby arrives. I understand that we are not of your village, but I know you welcome all and I'm thankful to be before you today. I humbly beg that you and your village and residents allow my niece to take refuge in your village, just to have her baby in peace, free of gossip and stress."

The chief sat quietly for a second and then finally spoke. "I can feel in my heart that this situation as it has been explained is much more stressful than we all can even imagine." He turned to his wife and his two staff members and nodded.

Chief Noumoury looked at Diaka. "My daughter, you are welcome in Oume, our village." He said to everyone in the room with a loud voice, "We have a new resident. Let's welcome her with a celebration. We will gather all the district villages at the Baobab tree at ten tomorrow morning to announce and welcome her."

Diaka let out a visible sigh of relief. They were welcoming her. She would get to live in this small village full of kind people until she delivered her child and could move back to the city to start her life over again.

When they returned to Poupette's house, they began preparing for sleep. Poupette brought her an extra blanket, as it had grown cold. "Tomorrow will be a big day, so get plenty of rest."

"What exactly is supposed to happen tomorrow? The chief said something about gathering at a tree?" Diaka had barely heard anything after they said she was welcome to stay.

Poupette laughed. "The chief has called a meeting to introduce you to the members of our community. There are about four hundred people in this village, but the chief oversees a whole district of surrounding villages, smaller than this one. The total amount of people is about eight hundred and fifty."

Diaka nodded. It was hard to imagine a community so small. Abidjan was a big, noisy, crowded city with six million people. A small neighborhood there had eight hundred and fifty people.

Poupette continued, "We'll meet at the tree in the center of our village. It's a beautiful place where the whole community comes together for special occasions like weddings and meetings, announcements and they also have a market there twice a week. You'll see everything in the morning. Get some rest."

But Diaka could hardly sleep. She had too many questions, thoughts, and worries. She finally decided to pray.

"Dear Heavenly Father, I humbly approach You, giving thanks for all You have done for me. Since I was a child, You watched over me. You saw me when I cried because I missed my mother. You were always there. You heard my cries when I felt I couldn't take care of my brothers and father and You gave me strength. Even my sins You have forgiven me and continue to bless me. Please give me strength as I meet the residents of my new home. I pray they will embrace me.

"God, I think of my father and brothers every day. I ask that You take care of them and continue to watch over them. I know one day the heart of my father will soften and he will accept me and my child—his grandchild. I also pray for Koffi. As You have forgiven me, I forgive him. I pray that one day he will have a change of heart and accept his child.

"You gave me a gift when my mother died. That gift is Aunt Namassa. She became more than my aunt; she became everything I needed her to be and more. I thank you for her. Please continue to bless her as she has been a loyal servant to You and a heartbeat for me when I felt my heart wasn't beating." She spoke to God well into the night, asking for His favor and His blessing and for Him to continue to guide the rest of her life.

The next morning, she awoke to the sound of drums beating in the distance. She knew in the village, drums were used to make announcements and wondered if it was about her. At almost 10 am, she heard the drums again.

Poupette came to the room to get her. "Those drums mean that the chief and his staff are going to the tree. We need to be leaving."

After walking a short distance on a dirt road crowded with many people, all staring at her and whispering, they reached a large clearing at the end of a row of houses. There was a humongous tree there whose branches shaded a large clearing area. The area was filled with people. Diaka could see people gathered in groups of ten or so around large pots. Poupette leaned to tell her, "The chief allocated food for the women of the village to prepare a breakfast for your meeting. Bread and rice pudding. You didn't eat at the house. Would you like to eat?"

Diaka frowned and shook her head. Her stomach was still too nervous.

The tree was larger than any she had ever seen, and its thick, strong branches provided shade for six to seven meters. There were beautiful wood seats decorated with colorful fabric around the base of the tree where Diaka guessed the chief and his staff would sit. Many elderly people sat around the base of the tree.

As she, Aunt Namassa, Poupette and Kaba approached, everyone began to look in her direction and whisper. Diaka wondered if the people would be as accepting of her as the chief and his staff. Would she be treated like she was in her neighborhood, with gossip, whispers, and stares?

The drum beat again and a long line of men in their traditional dress streamed from the chief's palace down the street. Women in colorful traditional dresses followed behind them. Diaka guessed they were the wives of the chief's staff and district heads.

The crowd parted to let them through. They took their seats in a semicircle at the base of the tree. The escort that had led them from Poupette's house sat them in a row of chairs not too far from the chief's staff.

The chief was announced. The entire crowd went completely silent as he began to speak. He addressed the crowd and thanked them for coming. Afterwards, he launched into Diaka's story. There was so much compassion in his voice that a tear trickled down Diaka's cheek. This man was treating her better than her father had.

She wiped the tear away. As the chief spoke, the villagers began looking at her with the same compassionate look in their eyes. There were no hard stares or judgmental frowns.

"I want to introduce her to you now." The chief gestured for her to come to where he was standing. "This is Diaka. I ask everyone to treat her like a sister, daughter, and friend and welcome her into our village and know that God will bless our village with positive things in the future for doing what we can for her. God just added a duty for every single one of us in this village. May God give us the means to accomplish the commitment we are accepting today to save these two lives for a better future for everyone tomorrow."

The chief lifted his hand and pointed across the street. "I've given her the house right across from our village center here. Please, the women will help to set up her house this afternoon. All of you, make sure she always has enough food to eat. Starting today, please treat her as one of our own."

Had Diaka heard correctly? He was giving her a house? She had already prepared to sleep on the floor in the room with Poupette's children for the next few months. She was going to have her own house. Her emotions swirled in her belly.

She looked around at the people of the village. As the chief finished talking, they began clapping and smiling, some cheering her name. The children were jumping up and down and waving at her. Some of the older women gathered in a group and began singing a song. Diaka didn't understand their dialect, but she heard her name in the song several times. Several youths gathered in a group and began singing and doing an energetic traditional dance.

What kind of village was this? What kind of people welcomed a stranger into their village and gave them a house and promised to keep them well fed? Tears streamed down Diaka's face. Chief Noumoury's wife, Gnale stood at her side and took her hand. Aunt Namassa took her other hand.

The people chanted her name. She couldn't stop crying. God had heard her prayers and had prepared a new life for her. He had forgiven her for her sins and proved to be a faithful God, no matter what she had done.

She would stay here and have her baby. As nice as these people were, maybe she would wait until the baby was a year old to move back to the city and start her life all over again.

Chapter 7

A big smile burst into Diaka's heart every time she thought of the day she was welcomed to Oume. She had to laugh at herself when she remembered planning to leave the village a year after she gave birth to go back to the city. It had been five years and she still lived in her little gifted house in Oume.

She swept the dirt path that led to her home. Her house was a simple, circular, mud brick house of two rooms that opened into a common area; one was the living area and the other was the bedroom she shared with her five-year-old son.

"Bamo, leave that chicken alone!" She yelled but laughed at her son chasing the fowl around the clearing area at the Baobab tree. He had become the greatest joy of her life. From the first time she laid eyes on him when he was born, she truly came to know what love really is.

She remembered his dedication ceremony a few months after he was born. The entire village and people from the surrounding villages came to celebrate with her under the Baobab tree. She cried when Aunty Namassa arrived with her brothers, Baba and Morris. She didn't expect to see them again and was grateful they were there to see her name her son after them–Baba and Morris gave her the combined name, Bamo.

They told her they would talk to her father and see if he would let her come home in a few months, but Diaka knew better. She was happy to see them and urged them to come back to visit with Aunt Namassa any time.

Watching Bamo grow up was like a dream. From the first smile, to the first tooth, to the first word, to the first step–every moment brought her intense joy.

She shook her head, watching him and the other village boys trying to corner the chicken near a tree. Bamo was such a fearless child and always kept her heart in her chest, hoping and praying his adventures wouldn't cause him to end up injured, or God forbid, dead. He climbed trees–the tallest ones–and liked to play on the highest, thinnest branches that looked like they would snap under his weight. She no longer allowed him to play with the boys near the river after he almost drowned venturing into water that was too deep.

The whole village kept an eye out for him and the mothers of Oume were always bringing him home, telling Diaka of his latest adventure. The men of Oume had all taken Bamo under their wings. Though refused by his natural father, he had many fathers–Chief Noumoury being the first and foremost. The chief's children were all older, and he and his wife, Gnale, acted as if Bamo was theirs.

Diaka and Bamo were well loved in Oume. She couldn't imagine them ever leaving.

Fabrice, the young boy who lived in the compound next door, ran up to her house. "Miss Diaka, do you need some more water? We're going to fetch today."

They had no electricity and no running water. In fact, to get good clean water, they often had to walk far, carrying a heavy basin on their heads. Most of the times, the young boys of the village fetched water for her. Diaka could barely lift a finger in the village without one of the young people taking over the task from her.

Diaka went to the water barrel in front of the house and opened it. "Yes, you could bring me some just for drinking. It's been raining so much that we've collected lots of rainwater. Thanks."

"You're welcome, Miss Diaka. Oh! My mother will come to

your house later. She's received a letter from her sister in the city and will need your help to read it."

Diaka nodded. "Okay, I'll be waiting for her."

Everyone in Oume and in the surrounding villages brought Diaka letters, official documents and any mail that needed reading. They used to walk six kilometers to the nearest town to have their letters read, but when Diaka moved to the village, they all came to her.

Her heart had broken when she first realized the problem of illiteracy in the group of farming villages. The people lived off the land and the closest government school was six kilometers away. The kids could walk, but education wasn't highly valued, so most of the parents had their children on the farms working rather than going to school.

After Diaka had realized the magnitude of the problem, she took it personally. She went from reading letters and documents to reading to the children in the evening under the Baobab tree. Then she started teaching them in the evenings under the tree. Their parents were excited that the educated woman from the city was teaching their children.

Pretty soon, Diaka convinced the parents to let their children come home from the farm early to come to her "school" under the tree. By the time the children came from a long day's work at the farm, it was hard for them to concentrate and learn. When they started coming in the afternoons, they were more alert and able to absorb knowledge.

Soon, she went from a gathering of children under a tree to a full school. When the chief saw that the children were learning to read, he commissioned the men of the village to build a large, one room school building. The mud brick building had twelve rows of wooden benches filled with children five days a week. Children also lined the floor around the benches and a small portion of the yard outside of the school.

Aunt Namassa brought two chalkboards and boxes and boxes of chalk from Abidjan. The children loved to draw on the board after class and the chalkboard had been instrumental in many of them learning to write their letters.

After the children got basic literacy and math skills, they began trekking to the government school in the neighboring town. Diaka hoped for the day when she could start a full-time school in their village.

All this had been accomplished by the help of some missionaries that Diaka was sure God had sent to their village. Jason and Stephanie Harrison were a young couple from America. A few years back, their car had broken down on the road right outside of Oume as they were traveling to a large town about a hundred kilometers away.

One of the boys from Oume brought them to the village. They were given food and a place to sleep and were showered with Oume hospitality. While they waited for the mechanic in the large town nearby to fix their car, they overheard Diaka teaching the kids in school. They visited the school that day and were excited about all Diaka had been able to accomplish with the children.

They delayed their trip for a week and stayed in Oume, helping to teach the kids and dreaming with Diaka about the school she wanted to build. Over the last three years since she had met them, they had brought over trunks full of books and learning materials.

Jason and Stephanie loved Bamo and brought him his own clothes, shoes, and books when they came over twice a year. On each visit, they taught him phrases in English. The whole village marveled at the fact that little Bamo could speak that funny sounding white man's language.

Bamo came running to her and threw himself around her legs. "Mummy, I want to go with the boys to play in the forest. Fabrice said he would watch me. Please!"

Diaka pulled her son off her legs and stared down into his little brown face. He looked just like his father. She laughed at the fact that Koffi could deny Bamo was his son because he looked as if Koffi had spit him out of his mouth.

"You already know my answer. No, Bamo. You know it's not safe in the forest. There's all sorts of animals and snakes there. Those boys shouldn't even be going."

"But I said please!"

She had been trying to reason with Bamo lately that saying please wasn't an automatic yes to whatever he asked her. He had learned well the lessons in manners she had taught him and all her students, but he seemed confused that good manners should always get him what he wanted.

"No, Bamo. You may not go."

Bamo began to cry and scream. In spite of all his goodness, he could be a stubborn, strong-headed child. The chief had advised her that when Bamo behaved so, she should just ignore him. If the stubbornness persisted, she should let the chief know. He believed that Bamo had a great spirit that shouldn't be broken, but carefully tamed. He always said that Bamo would be a great man and if some of his spirit was broken by a mother's discipline, he may not achieve all he was to accomplish in life.

Bamo continued screaming. When he first started throwing tantrums, he would kick and hit anything around him. Although Diaka respected what the chief said, she refused to have a child that hit and kicked to get his way. After a few gentle but firm strikes of a cane, he had resorted to only screaming.

"I don't want to hear your screaming today. Go into the room until you can behave like the good child I know you to be."

Bamo went to the bedroom, screaming and crying the whole way. His stubbornness caused him to scream for another ten minutes until Diaka threatened to call Chief Noumoury to deal with him. He quieted down and sat sullen in the room.

After sweeping the house, Diaka pulled some wood off her pile. Some boys kept her woodpile filled on a regular basis. The men of the village chopped firewood once a week, and the boys were careful to collect her enough to last. She took the wood back to her three-stone fire kitchen and built a small flame to begin cooking cassava and beef with palm nut oil.

It might seem strange that she had stayed so long in Oume. It was a small village with no water, electricity, or most of the comforts she had enjoyed in the city. But her life was simple and good. She had everything she needed and so much more. In the city, she might have comfort and convenience, but here, she was a part of a large family that loved her. And she was fulfilled changing the children's lives by giving them the gift of education.

She might not be successful by the world's standards, and it wasn't the life most people dreamed of, but it was a good life. She knew God was pleased with it, and she was too.

"Diaka, where are you?"

Diaka heard the voice of a young woman she had grown close to almost immediately when she came to Oume. Aicha had followed her around the village her first two days there and had insisted on helping her do any and everything that needed doing. Diaka had been immediately drawn to her, though she wasn't sure why.

A few days after she moved into her house, Aicha had come to visit. She offered to plait Diaka's hair for her. She was no longer wearing her stylish weaves from the city and her unruly, thick hair needed a style that could tame it. Aicha filled her head with beautiful, tiny braids in an intricate style. That became Diaka's signature hairstyle and Aicha was all too glad to spend the time with her every two weeks, putting the braids in.

On that first visit, Aicha had revealed that her mother had died when she was twelve, just like Diaka. Aicha was burdened with the care of her sick father and two younger brothers, just like Diaka. Diaka quickly became a mentor and big sister to Aicha. She had asked the chief to ask the girl's father for permission for Aicha to come and visit her often, and it had been granted. They had been inseparable for the past five years. Aicha was very close to Bamo as well.

"I'm back here in the kitchen," Diaka called out.

Aicha sauntered around the corner of the house with a big smile on her face.

"You're coming so early. Aren't you cooking today?" Diaka

asked. Saturday mornings were usually for cooking, doing laundry and cleaning the house. Just like in the city, except the chores were harder when one was trying to ration water and manage small amounts of cleaning products. They had to walk to town to get Omo and bleach. It was sold in the market at the Baobab tree, but the prices were much higher than in town.

"I woke up very early and finished my chores. And I didn't have to cook. Miss Grace brought over a pot of food." Aicha looked around from right to left to see if anyone was close enough to hear. She leaned in towards Diaka and said in a loud whisper, "I think she wants my father to marry her. You know she lost her husband in the great flood four years ago."

Every ten years or so, during a particularly heavy rainy season, there was terrible flooding in Oume and the surrounding villages. In the last flood, many had died from the heavy rains that persisted for ten to fourteen days. Chief Noumoury had lost his father, the great chief of the whole region, in a similar flood about twenty years ago.

Aicha grabbed a knife and started helping Diaka cook with a mischievous smile on her face. "For the last two months, Miss Grace has been cooking food and coming to check on my father and my brothers. I hope he does marry her. Then I don't have to do everything at home. And then maybe I can go to the city and go to school so I can be like you."

"Be like me how? Aren't I living in this village like you?" Diaka chuckled.

Ever since they had met, all Aicha dreamed about was going to the city to go to college and get a fancy job. After Aicha bothered and disturbed her so much about what life in the city was like, Diaka had told her some stories about her life before Oume. Aicha had become obsessed with Abidjan and was always looking for a way to release her burden of taking care of her family and escape to the city for the wonderful life she dreamed up.

The girl had grown so much since Diaka had taken her under her wing. She had learned to read and developed a voracious appetite for knowledge. Aicha read every single book Jason and Stephanie had ever brought over. Diaka had convinced Aunt Namassa to bring any book she could get her hands on when she came to visit once every month or so from Abidjan. Aicha served as Diaka's assistant in the school and was naturally gifted as a teacher.

Aicha fell in step with Diaka and they began cooking together, chatting about their students and the school and about the newest books Aicha had read. Aunt Namassa had snuck a couple romance books into her latest delivery. Aicha was telling the characters' love story with a dreamy look in her eyes like they were real people.

"One day, I'm going to have a husband that will take me all over the world." Aicha let out a deep sigh. "Diaka, don't you ever want to get married? You never talk about it. And all the men of the village that approach you, you refuse. Why?"

Diaka stirred her pot slowly, thinking of an answer. When she first met Aicha, the girl was only sixteen. But she had grown into quite an intelligent and mature young woman, because of having to take care of her family, but the reading and learning had also grown her up and expanded her world.

Diaka answered, "I guess I haven't seen any man I would want to marry. And Bamo's such a handful. He's enough for me right now."

Aicha frowned. "Are you sure that's all it is?"

The girl was too wise for her own good. Diaka nodded and added some salt to her pot. She wasn't about to tell Aicha that she still remembered the look on Koffi's face when he refused her and their child. And she still remembered the look on her father's face when he disowned her. She wasn't interested in giving her heart to any man. Probably ever.

Diaka changed the subject. The women began dreaming of the bigger school they wanted to build and other things they wanted to do for the village. They had just finished cooking when they heard a scream from the compound next door.

They ran over to the neighbor's house. Two of the older boys were carrying Fabrice in their arms. His body was limp. Diaka stared in horror as they pointed to a large, swollen wound on his leg.

"A viper bit him. Call the traditional medicine man."

But it was too late for herbs. Fabrice's eyes were open and glassy. Diaka recognized the look of death on his young face.

His mother screamed and wailed so loud; it drew the attention of anyone in the village who hadn't gone to the farm. All came screaming and wailing.

Diaka wailed and cried with all of them. Fabrice had been her helper since she moved into her house, always fetching water and bringing wood and anything else she needed. How could he be dead at eleven years old?

Diaka watched Fabrice's mother writhing on the ground. She couldn't imagine what it felt like to lose a son. Thank God Bamo hadn't gone to the forest with the boys.

Bamo.

Where was he? Diaka hadn't heard a peep from him since banishing him to his room. She knew he couldn't still be sitting there and assumed he had gone to the chief's palace or to play with any of his other many friends in the village.

She ran to her house. "Bamo? Where are you?" As she expected, he wasn't in the room.

As the villagers were streaming toward her neighbor's house, Diaka was running to every house she knew of where Bamo might be playing. It was a lot of houses because Bamo was welcome and well-loved in every single home. As she ran from house to house, not seeing her son, her heart filled with panic.

Bamo usually wasn't one to disobey, but twice, he had directly disobeyed her and done the opposite of what she told him. She hoped today wasn't a third time.

She continued running from house to house, but every house was either empty because people were at the farm or had run to her neighbor's house to see what was happening. Diaka ran back to her compound and still didn't see her son. She was crying and wailing, but not for the same reason everyone else had. Had Bamo snuck out and followed the boys? Had he been bitten by a snake before they even saw that he was there with them?

She ran back to her neighbor's house. Her heart filled with relief when she saw Bamo there, sitting on the chief's lap. His face was filled with tears. He was clinging to the chief. She ran and scooped him into her arms.

"Bamo! Where were you? I thought you had gone to the forest."

"Mummy, why would I go to the forest when you told me not to?" He looked confused and scared.

"Yes, my son. Yes." She held him tight to her chest and cried. She was overwhelmed at the fact that she could have lost her sweet son. He was all she had in this life and the thought of losing him caused her heart to break inside.

"Mummy, what will Mami Fabrice do without her son?"

Diaka shook her head and held him tighter. "I don't know, my love. I don't know."

Chapter 8

"But where would we get the teachers from?" Diaka's forehead wrinkled in frustration.

"Don't worry about that. Just tell me about your plan. Let me hear the plan and then we'll figure out all the specifics." Stephanie's smiling face held such a peace and calm that it made Diaka almost believe all this dreaming they were doing could actually happen.

Jason and Stephanie were in Oume on one of their twice-yearly trips. They always tried to time one of their trips around Bamo's birthday celebrations. He had turned six a few days ago, and they had a huge celebration under the Baobab tree for him. They had even slaughtered a goat to roast. It was one of the rare occasions when Diaka got to eat meat. Gone were the days when she was making money and could eat meat several times a week. Now it only happened on special occasions, a few times a year.

"Diaka, just tell us your plan. Let us worry about where the money and teachers will come from." Stephanie translated for Jason. She was fluent in French, but even after taking a class on the computer, he couldn't even put a sentence together. Stephanie had to translate for him at all times when he was in the Ivory Coast.

Diaka wrinkled her nose. "I don't have a plan really. I just want to build a real school in this village. I want it so the kids don't have to walk six kilometers to town. I want every child in this village and in the surrounding villages educated. I want them to have a better life than they have right now."

As much as she loved her simple life in the village, the poverty was heartbreaking. Seeing kids wear the same worn clothes or no clothes at all and no shoes year after year seemed like such an injustice. She didn't have much when she was growing up in Abidjan, but this felt a hundred times worse.

It wasn't only the children that couldn't afford clothes. Most people couldn't. They'd wear the same worn shirts, pants, and dresses day after day and year after year until they were threadbare and dingy. Many in the village couldn't afford to eat every day. Fortunately, some families, after a good harvest, donated to the village food bank so they could share with those that didn't have food. The chief and his staff were responsible for evenly distributing the food to the villagers. Sometimes there would be a long line of people waiting outside the food storage just hoping there would be enough for them to eat.

Clean water was also a big issue. Rainwater could be used for washing and cleaning, but there was never enough clean water to drink. Children died from diarrhea all the time from diseases they got from drinking bad water.

Diaka felt that somehow, education was the cure for their poverty. She wasn't sure how, but surely, educating the children would help them come up with solutions to all the issues they faced in Oume.

Diaka shrugged. "All I know is, children should have access to a good education. They should have more choices than farming...or farming."

"But Diaka, what will they do with all this education?" Sory asked. He was a part of the chief's staff and always seemed to be against Diaka's plans for educating the children. Diaka wondered why the chief always sent him as a representative in anything having to do with her school.

"You'll educate the children, but there are no jobs in this village other than farming." Sory frowned. "Should we educate them all so they can move to the city and compete with all the young people there that already can't find jobs? I appreciate the things you've been teaching them so far. It's good for them to know math for when they need to take their crops to the market. Maybe what we should be teaching them is better farming methods."

He turned to Jason and Stephanie. "Can you bring in teachers for that? Better farming? Can't we use the money you're talking of bringing over to build this school for a new irrigation system? Why are we wasting money on books when that's not what this village needs?"

Diaka bit her tongue. What could she say? She knew the high unemployment rate among educated youth in the larger cities on the Ivory Coast. Her parents had taught her to believe that an education was a way out of poverty, but the life she was living right now wasn't exactly the best example of that.

Stephanie glared at Sory, but spoke to Diaka, "Ok, right now, you're teaching them the basics–the alphabet, numbers, basic reading and writing and basic math. Are you teaching any of the sciences or social studies?"

Diaka shook her head.

"The only science they need is how to grow crops," Sory said. "Or even better, let them learn how to build a dam so the river doesn't overflow its banks in rainy season. That would really help this village. Not to flood in heavy downpours. Do you know how many crops we lose due to rain?"

Stephanie gave that smile she gave when she didn't like something but was pretending to like it. Diaka knew the smile from when Stephanie was trying to convince someone that something about their village life was okay with her when it wasn't. "Why don't we just stop for today? I'm ready to eat anyway. Maybe we can meet again in a few days?"

Diaka nodded and stood. She was also ready to end this meeting. It was going nowhere. They said their goodbyes, and she followed Stephanie and Jason to the chief's house where they stayed when they visited. As soon as they were in sight distance of the palace, Bamo came barreling out of the door and ran straight into Jason's arms.

"Bamo!"

"Mr. Jason!"

Even though Bamo was six, Jason picked him up and sat him on his shoulders as he had done since Bamo was two years old. They started speaking English to each other. Diaka smiled. She was proud that her son could speak English, but it bothered her a bit that it was a part of his world she didn't fit into.

She should get used to it though. For the past two years, Jason and Stephanie had been asking to take Bamo to America for schooling and for a "better life." She wouldn't hear of her son leaving her, even though they tried to convince her that would be the best for him. She had finally agreed that he could go to university in the US. Stephanie had started hinting that for him to get accepted to a good university, it would be best for him to do high school in America. Diaka had about eight years before she had to make that decision.

Stephanie and Diaka walked behind Jason and Bamo towards the chief's palace.

Stephanie spoke a mixture of French and the Mandingo she'd been learning. "Diaka, I really want you to think about what kind of school you want to build and what you would need to build it. There's money out there for projects like this. In fact, there's a grant I saw recently that would help greatly with a school project. We can appeal to mission programs for French-speaking missionaries and university programs for French majors to come teach. This is really possible. I need you to think about it and write up information to help me write a grant and proposals. Can you do that?"

Diaka nodded, even though she knew nothing of writing grants and proposals. She had written many documents for Koffi to submit when she worked in his office so she knew she could write something. It just might not be exactly what Stephanie was asking for.

As if she read her thoughts, Stephanie said, "It doesn't have to be perfect. Just send me enough information to work with and I'll put it in grant proposal form."

Diaka nodded. "Thanks. I appreciate everything you do for me. And for Oume. God will reward you richly."

Only God could pay Jason and Stephanie back for all they had done for Oume, for her school and for Bamo. They brought suitcases of clothes and good shoes over twice a year for the children. They brought books and school supplies that the school couldn't run without. They brought boxes of medications that had saved lives in the village. They were working towards building a small medical clinic and had started trying to figure out how to bring a constant supply of clean water to Oume and the surrounding villages.

In addition to meeting needs, they also brought Bamo toys and things. Unfortunately, Bamo kept very little of what Stephanie and Jason brought him. He was always giving away his clothes and shoes to his friends. He never played with his toys alone and often gave them away to his favorite friends in the village.

The only thing he didn't share was the candy they brought him. He'd keep it stashed for months, eating one piece a day before going to sleep. He sat with the candy for a while, staring at it before eating it. Then he'd lick it and lick it, over and over again. It could take him two hours to eat one small piece. Diaka always laughed at him and called him selfish because he wouldn't even share the candy with her.

Diaka didn't always like how much Jason and Stephanie spoiled Bamo. They also put ideas in his head about this great future ahead of him. They brought their white man ideas and dreams and were infecting her son with it. What would she do with him when he grew up, expecting all the things they told him to come true?

"Diaka, it's not safe for you to go to town. What are you thinking?"

"Stephanie said I had to have the proposal for the school to her by tomorrow. If I miss the deadline, then she can't turn in the grant and we don't get the money. It's important that I email it to her before tomorrow."

It had been two months since Stephanie and Jason left. Diaka had been working on the information Stephanie had asked her for, but it was much harder and took much longer than she thought it would. She had worked on it right up until the deadline Stephanie gave her and still didn't feel like it was as good as it needed to be.

"Diaka, you're talking about money for a school, but your life is at stake. It's been raining for ten days straight now. This is the worst rain we've had in years. The river is surely flooding town. It's not safe for you to go."

Aicha was always fearful about things without cause. Diaka was overprotective when it came to Bamo, but Aicha was overprotective about everybody and everything. Diaka thought it was because of the way Aicha's mother had died. And honestly, the way many died in the village. People were always getting sick, or having accidents, or just dropping dead for unexplainable reasons, and it seemed like death came too easy.

But Diaka wasn't going to let Aicha's constant fears keep her from connecting with Stephanie. Before she left, Stephanie had challenged her to really dream about the school. And dream she had. Now it was all she thought about. A larger school building, missionary teachers coming in that could teach other subjects than math and reading, more books, better school supplies–everything they needed to educate the children from all the district villages.

Bamo had learned so much, he wouldn't be able to stay in her school for much longer. Even though she knew it was normal for the children of Oume, she didn't want him walking six kilometers to school every day. Chief said she pampered Bamo too much but walking that far wasn't something she wanted him to have to do.

She had to get to Stephanie. If they were awarded the grant, the money would be given in six months. They could begin building by early next year. They could ship a container of supplies, books, clothes, and shoes a few months later. And they could start receiving the missionary teachers in time for the next school year, starting in September. Diaka dreamed about it all day long.

She rushed around her room, putting her notes together and gathering things she would need for the walk to town. She decided to take enough money for two hours on the Internet. With the slow Internet, it might take that long. And she didn't want to be rushed. She would have to put the papers inside something because it was raining heavily, and she didn't have an umbrella. She rummaged through her suitcase and found an old plastic bag she had packed years ago when she came to Oume. She hoped it would hold up.

"What's this?" Aicha picked up a small brown wallet that had fallen out of Diaka's suitcase.

"Oh my goodness! Did I drop that? Please, bring it here. I need to put it somewhere safe." Diaka almost snatched the worn wallet she had taken from her mother's things years ago. It was the same wallet her mother had stored the necklace in that she gave her.

"What is it?" Aicha looked a little hurt and Diaka was sorry she had snatched the wallet.

"Sorry. It's from my mother. She gave it to me the day before she died." Diaka opened the wallet and took out the gold necklace her mother had given her. She felt her heart pang. All these years later and she still felt the pain of her death deep in her soul. She held up the necklace for Aicha to see.

"My family has passed this down to the firstborn child for more than one hundred years."

Diaka explained about the lion and the bull on the necklace and then tucked it back into the wallet. She put the wallet back into her suitcase. She'd have to find somewhere safer to keep it. She couldn't bear the thought of anything happening to it.

Diaka put her notes in the plastic bag and brought out her rain boots Stephanie gave her on her last visit. They were a blessing and would make her walk to town much easier.

"Diaka! You're not listening to me. You can't go to town. You've only been in Oume for six years, so you've never seen it when it floods. I've lived here all my life and I'm telling you, you can't go."

Diaka pulled Aicha close and kissed her cheek. She understood the fearfulness that came into a person's life when they lost their mother at a young age. It was only Aunt Namassa that kept her from being the same way. "Aicha, you'll keep an eye on Bamo for me. I left some palm nut soup in the kitchen that he can eat with rice. That is, if he comes home from the chief's house. I can never get him out of there."

"Diaka! I'm going to tell the chief that you're trying to walk to town in this rain. You know his father died in the flood, so he'll agree with me."

"Sure, go tell him. In fact, he may send one of his messengers to escort me. I'll wait here for you."

Diaka waited until Aicha had completely disappeared into the fog and rain before she left the house to make the long walk to town. She needed to hurry and go so she could get there, type the document, and come back before nightfall. She was well known in town and could easily stay with someone overnight, but she wanted to be back in her own house with her son.

As she started walking towards town, she laughed at Aicha's fears. It was wet and muddy and the gutters along the side of the road had a small river flowing swiftly towards the village, but it wasn't dangerous. Her boots got stuck in the mud a few times, but it wasn't nothing life threatening.

As she walked along, the rain seemed to get heavier and heavier. It beat down on her back in weighty pellets. She quickened her pace and pulled her rain jacket tighter around her. She tucked the plastic bag with her notes into her skirt to keep it dry. It wouldn't do to reach town only to find the notes completely soaked and unable to read.

She smiled to herself as she thought of her school. It would be wonderful. Maybe if they had really great teachers, Bamo wouldn't have to go to America for high school. He could stay in

Oume at her school until university and she wouldn't have to lose her son. Her whole life. She knew she had to let go of him one day, but the longer she could hold on to him, the better.

After about three kilometers of walking, Diaka looked ahead and saw people running toward her. She frowned and tried to understand what they were yelling to her. The first person reached her screaming but didn't stop. He ran past her. The next woman came running toward her screaming in Mandingo. The woman grabbed her arm and pulled Diaka to run with her.

"What's happening? What's wrong?"

Her screaming was so high pitched and panicked, Diaka didn't understand the woman well. After a few moments, she didn't have to understand. She heard it and then immediately felt it. Crashing waves of freezing cold water rushed over her. It came so fast, Diaka's feet lifted off the ground and flipped over her head. She screamed and felt water rushing into her mouth. She choked. She flailed and fought.

And then she prayed. "Father, help me."

She fought the water, but it was too strong and too cold. There was nothing she could do. She felt a wave of peace wash over her. It was warm and strong and overpowered the coldness of the water. She felt the warmth begin to overtake every part of her. It had a familiar feeling to it. It felt like her mother's smile. It was as if she could feel her mother's soft hands on her scalp. She could hear her singing their song with her heart. She saw her father's face smiling at her, telling her how proud he was of her. She saw her brothers playing football outside their family compound, laughing as if they didn't have a care in the world.

She saw the day she was welcomed to the village. She saw the day she gave birth to her son and her heart burst with joy. She saw him running and playing in the village.

That's what it felt like. Warm joy. She smiled. "Bamo...I love you..."

Her mother's singing got louder and louder until that was all she could hear. And then...she felt her mother's embrace.

PART II

BAMO

Chapter 9

B amo woke up with a start. He'd had another dream. He'd been having them for the last eight years since his mother died. He used to have them all the time, but now, he only had them about once a year, when it was time for his house changing ceremony.

He remembered that night like it was yesterday. He sat in the house with Aicha, waiting for his mother to come home. Aicha said she had gone to town—that going was dangerous. The chief and half the village gathered around their little house in the mud. His mother never came home.

A man had come to the village the next morning with the bad news. He had been on the road from town the night before and ran past Diaka when she was going to town. He tried to yell and tell her not to go, but she kept walking. A few minutes later, the river had swept over the road. He was able to climb up a tree but saw Diaka and another woman being swept away.

The whole village gathered at the Baobab tree to hear the news. The drummers beat out a sorrowful rhythm to let the other villages of the district know. People didn't gather as they normally would have because it was still raining.

Two weeks later, after the rain had stopped, they had a proper funeral for Diaka. Bamo remembered it as the saddest day of his life. The whole clearing around the Baobab tree and the road leading to the village were all packed with people coming to pay their respects.

The chief and his wife, Gnale, could barely speak, and it was the chief's assistant who spoke of all the wonderful things Diaka had done for their village in her years there. Bamo remembered clinging to Aicha's hand. She never stopped crying the whole day.

It was then that Bamo met his uncles for who he was named. They kept trying to hold him and speak to him, but he didn't know them. He kept running back to the chief's lap and to lay his head on Mama Gnale's bosom. His mother's aunt Namassa was there, and she kept crying for her Diaka and her Jeneba. Bamo only came to understand later that his great aunt was crying about his mother and her mother, both who had died too young.

He had seen his aunt over the years, many times when she came to visit every few months to visit Diaka. She always brought him biscuits and rubbed his cheeks and spoke sweet words over him.

When the funeral was over, Aunt Namassa and his uncles, Baba and Morris came to the chief. Bamo couldn't understand what was happening when the chief began telling him he was to go with these strangers. They made a big ceremony over turning him back over to his family.

When he finally understood that he was supposed to leave the village, the only home he had ever known, he ran. Bamo ran as fast as his little legs could take him down the main village road and straight into the forest where his mother had forbidden him to go. He didn't care if he was bitten by a viper or attacked by a lion as his mother had always warned him.

In fact, he hoped for it. Then he could die and go be with his mother in this place called heaven where Aicha said she had gone to. He didn't understand what could be so great about this place called heaven that would make his mother want to leave him to go there. And if she wanted to go so bad, then why didn't she take him with her? Why would she leave him alone in Oume, while she got to enjoy heaven?

He hid in the forest all night, hoping and praying for a viper to come and bite him, but none ever did. The next morning, he got hungry and hobbled back to the village. When the first people saw him, they screamed and ran straight to the chief's palace, shouting his name. The whole village came out shouting and crying. They thought he had died in the forest.

One man picked him up and carried him straight to the chief's palace. When the chief saw him he grabbed him and held him tight. Mama Gnale wrapped her arms around the both of them and they all cried.

"Please don't make me go with those people. Please let me stay here in Oume. Please don't make me leave Oume."

He begged over and over, crying until he was tired. He fell asleep, crying in Chief's arms.

The next day, he woke up to Mama Gnale's smiling face hovering over him. He jumped up into her arms and began his cries again. "Please don't make me go."

"Shush, child. Your aunt and uncles have left. They were very worried about you. Don't ever disappear like that again. You could have been killed by..." Mama Gnale's face darkened as she seemed to swallow her words. She shook her head. "Anything could have happened to you." She held Bamo tight in her arms.

"Are they coming back for me?" Bamo's heart was filled with terror. The thought of going to the big city with those strangers made him want to run for the forest again. He'd take his chances there.

"No, my dear. They decided that for now, it's best to leave you here with us. Your Aunt Namassa knows how much your mother loved this village. Your mother always said that Oume saved her life and your life, too. Oume became her family, and she loved this village with her whole life. She gave her life trying to help this village. It meant that much to her."

Bamo buried his face in Mama Gnale's chest and cried. "Thank you, Mama. Thank you. I want to stay in Oume with my family. I want to stay in this village my mother loved."

"Yes, dear. After you ran, and we decided that you will stay in Oume, so many people came forward, wanting to take you in. Everybody in the village wants the chance for you to live with them. Your mother is well loved in Oume. She did so much for this village, and everybody wants to pay her back by taking care of you. We were so overwhelmed by the response that we're trying to decide what to do."

Bamo sat up in his bed, remembering that day, more than eight years ago, when his fate had been decided. The day after his mother's funeral, all of Oume had gathered under the Baobab tree. Many families were giving their request for Bamo to come live with them. Bamo cried and cried as he saw how much the people loved him.

The chief had decided the whole village would take care of Bamo. He would live with Chief and Mama Gnale for the first year and then every year, he would go to a new family. Everyone would have a chance to love and take care of Bamo.

Every year, they had a big celebration under the Baobab tree as Bamo moved on to the next family. The whole village celebrated him. As the family he was leaving wept, the family he was joining rejoiced. Every year, they recounted Diaka's works for the village and how she had been a great blessing to all of Oume. They celebrated her memory and everything she had meant to them.

Everyone in Oume and all the village districts well-loved and well-knew Bamo. He could eat or sleep at any house at any time and he had many friends he played with. Even though he was sad his mother was gone, he was glad that he was going to stay in Oume with all the people he loved.

It sounded like a good idea at the time—being loved by so many different families, but at age eleven, Bamo was tired. Tired of going from house to house. Tired of being met by jealous children when he moved into a new house. Tired of fathers who looked at him as if he didn't belong in their house.

Some of the kids in the village were jealous of him because he had lots of nice clothes, shoes, books, and toys that Stephanie and Jason continued to bring him twice a year. After his mother died, they had argued with the chief that they should be allowed to take Bamo to America. Chief had said that it was his mother's desire that he stay in Oume, but Jason and Stephanie argued that was only because Diaka wanted Bamo there with her. Now that she was gone, Diaka would have wanted him to go to America for a better life and a better education.

Bamo loved Jason and Stephanie and was very happy when they came twice a year for their visits, but when he heard the argument that they wanted to take him away from Oume to a strange, white man country where everyone spoke the funny language Jason was teaching him, he ran away and spent another night in the forest.

Jason and Stephanie were always talking of the life they wanted to give him in America. He'd have his own bedroom in their house. He'd go to a good school. He'd have good food every day with meat and vegetables and would always have good clean water. He'd have good clothes and for those times when he fell sick each year, he'd have access to good medical care rather than having to drink the medicine man's bitter herbs.

In addition to being jealous about all the wonderful things Bamo had from America, most of the kids were jealous that Bamo would get to go live there one day. The kids were also jealous that he was the smartest child in school. He always took number one in class. When Jason and Stephanie came, they gave him the most attention.

Bamo tried to make the other kids like him more. He gave away many of his toys and clothes. Sometimes he gave away his shoes. Although the last time Mr. Jason came and found him running barefoot, he was angry with him. He knew Mr. Jason was trying not to look angry, but he knew that he was. He tried to explain in English that the kids didn't like him. That they thought their parents treated them better than they when he lived in their houses.

Mr. Jason just kept telling him that he was special and not to worry about the other kids. That was easy for him to say. He didn't have to live in the village.

Bamo missed his mother. He never thought anything could hurt so bad as her not being there. Not being able to see her smile or feel her arms around him. He even missed her scolding at him and pulling his ear when he was naughty. He most missed the way she sang him that special song her mother used to sing to her when she was a girl. Before her mother died.

Maybe that's why his mother left him and went to heaven so early. Maybe she missed her mother as much as he was missing her. If Bamo could figure out a way to get to heaven, he would surely go. Just to be with his precious Mummy again.

One day after school, he went and hid in his favorite hiding place—a large tree at the edge of the forest. He went there when he was missing his mother most. To think about her and cry until his heart didn't feel like a heavy rock had been dropped on it. He would hold his head back and sing. He sang her song towards heaven, hoping she would hear him. Maybe she would come back to him. Or maybe she would send for him like her mother had sent for her.

He heard a rustling in the bushes. He froze. He wasn't far enough in the forest that there should be a lion or any other dangerous creature there. It was Emmanuel, an older boy Bamo had lived with last year. He and his brothers hated Bamo and said their mother beat them more while he was around, always asking them, "Why can't you be smart and well-behaved like Bamo?"

His brothers, Franck and Wilfred, were with him, and two other older boys from the village. Bamo had given Yves his best truck from Jason and his favorite red t-shirt, but the boy still hated him.

"Bamo, Bamo, orphan Bamo. Mother stealer, American boy, Bamo, Bamo." Emmanuel sang his taunting song he had started singing the first week after Bamo started living with them. The boys had caused so much trouble that Bamo moved on to the next house not even two months after moving in with them. They didn't even have a celebration under the Baobab tree. He was just quietly transferred to the next house. Emmanuel's mother hung her head in shame for a few months after that. Bamo's time at her house had been a failure. She felt embarrassed among the other women in the village.

All five boys surrounded Bamo in a circle, singing that taunting song. Bamo was afraid. Emmanuel had beat him up twice while he was staying in their house. The first time, the chief told him to work things out with the boy. The second time, Emmanuel had beaten Bamo so badly that he went and spent the night in the forest. When he came back, Chief Noumoury had already had his things moved to the next house.

"Singing boy. Singing that sad song. Let me teach you how to be a man." Emmanuel was snarling at him with hatred in his eyes.

"Please, what have I done? Please, leave me alone." Bamo's voice was shaky and so high, he sounded like a girl.

The boys laughed. "What have you done? What have you done? You don't know?" Emmanuel circled him, staring at him.

Bamo wished the ground would open up and swallow him. He turned to Wilfred, Emmanuel's youngest brother. "Please, Wilfred. Please."

Wilfred was only two years older than Bamo. They were friends in school before Bamo moved into their house.

"Shut your mouth!" Emmanuel shouted, looking at his brother in warning. It was Wilfred that had run to get their mother that first day Emmanuel was beating Bamo to make him stop. Wilfred looked at the ground.

Emmanuel sang his taunting sang, taking steps closer and closer to Bamo until Bamo's nose was on his chest. Bamo stood frozen. He was fast, one of the fastest boys in the village, but didn't think he could outrun all of them.

Emmanuel took a step back and slammed his fist into the side of Bamo's head. Bamo saw stars and fell to the ground. Emmanuel kicked him in his side. He curled up in a ball as Emmanuel kicked him and kicked him, in his head, in his back, his legs. Bamo could hear the other boys cheering him on.

Then the jeers were replaced by screams. Bamo's head felt like it had doubled in size and he couldn't see straight so he didn't understand what was happening. But the pain stopped. He lifted his head in time to see Emmanuel and the other boys running away. He laid his head back on the ground and cried.

He felt arms lifting him and heard a voice that was vaguely familiar. "Bamo, Bamo. Sorry eh. Sorry eh..."

He groaned as he looked out of swollen eyes to see a face. It was Caleb. Caleb was from the next village over. It was Caleb's mother that was swept away in the flood with his own mother. The boy had come to see him to say sorry about his mother dying. Bamo thought that strange because the boy's mother had died, too.

He saw Caleb all the time when he left his mother's small school in the village and walked the six kilometers to town to go to the larger school there. Caleb was always in trouble. He was a very wild boy, and Bamo wondered why he was even in school most days. He made noise, picked fights, and talked to himself in the back of the classroom.

Many of the kids said he went mad or was bewitched when his mother died. Bamo didn't think so though. If Caleb's heart hurt as much as his did, the boy's behavior made sense. Perfect sense.

He looked up at Caleb. "How did you get rid of them?"

Caleb held up a slingshot and a big smile crossed his face as he pointed up to a high branch on the tree. "Stones soaked in pepper and limestone."

Caleb tried lifting him, but every time he moved him, Bamo cried out in pain. "Oh, Bamo, I can't carry you now. Should I bring someone from your village?"

Bamo turned his head to Caleb. "Please. Leave me here to die." He stared into Caleb's eyes. They were like a mirror. He saw the same bitter pain he felt.

Caleb nodded and sat down next to him. Then he frowned. "No, you can't die."

Bamo stared at him. If anybody could understand, he could. Caleb held his head in his hands. "After my mother died...our mothers died... I drank poison. I tried to die. My grandmother was very upset and cried and cried while the medicine man gave me medicine to drink. After I was better, she told me that my mother would be very mad if I showed up in heaven so soon after her. She said my mother would be angry at me for the rest of eternity for coming to heaven too early."

Caleb stared into Bamo's eyes. "Do you believe your mother is in heaven?"

Bamo nodded and winced. The slight movement caused his head to pain.

"Then you can't die. Your mother will be mad at you for all of eternity if you go there now."

Bamo closed his eyes and began to cry.

"Sorry, Bamo. Just manage the pain, okay?" Caleb picked Bamo up and put him over his shoulder. Caleb was a few years older than he and a bit bigger, but Bamo didn't know how long he could carry him. The pain of every step Caleb took became too much and Bamo passed out.

He woke up to familiar surroundings. It was his bedroom at the chief's house. Mama Gnale sat over him with a cool rag on his forehead. His clothes had been changed and he could smell the herbal antiseptic used for cuts and wounds. His head felt drowsy and his mouth tasted bitter, so he knew the medicine man had been there. He tried to sit up but every part of his body hurt.

"Be still, Bamo. Don't try to move. Just be still. Who did this to you?"

Bamo shook his head. If he told, Emmanuel would only find him and beat him again.

"Bamo, the chief will come to ask you and you will have to tell him. The person who did this must be handled."

Bamo looked around the room. "Where's Caleb? The boy that brought me here."

"Nobody brought you here. Mr. Zaba found you at the Baobab tree. Who is Caleb?"

Bamo shook his head again. He knew Caleb didn't want to be known. He might be good with a slingshot in a tree, but at school, the boys would corner him and beat him well.

"Bamo, all these secrets. Tell me who brought you to the village and tell me who did this to you?"

Bamo turned his head away from Mama Gnale and squeezed his eyes shut. He heard her clicking her tongue. He lay there ignoring her questions until he drifted off to sleep again.

The next morning, he woke up to find Chief Noumoury sitting at his bedside. "Bamo, how are you feeling?"

"Fine, sir." He knew he couldn't get away with not answering the chief.

"Gnale says you don't want to talk about what happened. I'll only ask this. Emmanuel came home from school late yesterday with an open, bleeding wound on his head. Does that have anything to do with what happened to you?"

A tear slid down Bamo's face. His only hope was to plead with the chief. "Please sir, if you say anything, he'll only beat me again. This is the third time. If it hadn't been for Caleb, he would have killed me yesterday."

Chief grunted. "So I should leave a murderer to be free in Oume? One that would murder Bamo, son of Diaka?"

"Please, sir," Bamo pleaded, a tear slipping down his face.

"I will handle it." The chief said it with such finality that Bamo knew not to speak again. "A young man came early this morning asking after you. I believe him to be the young man whose mother died with yours?"

Bamo nodded. "Caleb. He was the one that ran off Emmanuel and the boys that attacked me. He brought me back to the village. He saved me."

"He told me talk to you. Bamo, did you ask him to leave you there to die?"

Bamo closed his eyes and turned away from the chief. Tear slipped from under his closed lids down his face. He hated crying in front of the chief, but he couldn't stop the tears from flowing.

Chief Noumoury put one of his large hands on Bamo's arm. "Bamo, why would you say such a thing?"

Bamo just shook his head.

Chief Noumoury let out a deep breath. "You know many years

ago a great flood took my father's life. I was older than you were when I lost my father but I..."

Chief paused and tried to shake Bamo's arm to get him to open his eyes. "You'll be fine, Bamo. You see how I ended up being a great chief of these villages. You're going to be a great man, too. One day, when the memory is not so strong that you feel it every day, you will see your greatness. I can see it. Everyone in the village can see that you will be great. Some of us celebrate your greatness. Others try to kill it. But, Bamo, you will be great."

Bamo shrugged. "I don't want to be a chief. I don't want to be a great man. I just want my mother back."

"Bamo, if I could bring our Diaka back I would. Sometimes our greatness comes as a result of great pain. When you seek to overcome the thing that tried to kill you, that's when you become great. Always remember that. Your greatness lies in the very thing that tried to destroy you. You'll remember that, my son?"

Bamo nodded. He had no idea what the chief was talking about, he just wanted him to stop talking so his head wouldn't hurt. "Yes, sir."

The chief patted his arm. "This Emmanuel. Why is he after you?"

Bamo sucked his teeth. "It started when I lived in his house. He thought his mother treated me better than him. I've had lots of problems in the homes where I've lived. I didn't want to complain because people are so good to take care of me, but..."

The chief waited. Bamo sat up in bed. It pained him to do so, but he wanted to present his request as respectfully as possible.

"Easy, son. Rest now."

"Chief, please. Please, I don't want to live with the families in the village anymore. I have no home. When I was with my mother, I had a home. I had love. I knew she cared for me. Sometimes, the people here..."

"Yes, son?"

Bamo didn't want to speak badly of anyone. "Everyone loved my mother very much. I just...please, Chief. I don't want to keep moving around anymore. Can I...can I please stay here with you and Mama Gnale? Please?"

"Of course, son. We were trying to give a chance for everyone to take care of you. To return some of the love your mother poured out on this village. But you know this is your first home. Me and Gnale love you as if you're ours. You can move back here and stay until you're an old man."

Bamo laughed. "Not until I'm an old man, Chief. Just until..."

"Just until when, Bamo?"

"I don't know, Chief. Just until..."

Chapter 10

Chief Noumoury had Bamo's things moved to his house that day, and he'd lived with them ever since. Bamo didn't know what he said to Emmanuel, but one day, after he was feeling much better, Emmanuel was brought to the chief's palace by his contrite mother and his father. They both apologized to Bamo in front of the chief's counsel. Emmanuel was forced to apologize again.

Bamo could only imagine the beating the boy was given by his parents. His mother spoke of her shame at what her son had done to Bamo. Emmanuel must have been sharply warned because he had never so much as looked at Bamo again. He no longer came to school and was at the farm with his family every day. His brother Franck was also withdrawn from school and sent to the farm. Wilfred still came to the school. He stayed far away from Bamo until one day, Bamo shared a piece of goat meat with him. They had been friends since.

Wilfred, Caleb and Bamo were the best of friends and spent every waking moment together, in and out of school. Bamo spent many hours tutoring Caleb and helping him catch up in school. Caleb was always taking Bamo on an adventure or teaching him some skill. He taught him to be an expert marksman with the slingshot. He taught him to kill bush meat in the forest that the three boys skinned, cleaned, roasted over an open fire and then ate until they were almost sick. He taught him how to play football because Bamo had two left feet.

They raced almost every day, even though Bamo always won.

He was uncoordinated when it came to football, but he was fast. The fastest in the whole school. They built a small treehouse with bamboo shoots and palm fronds in their favorite big tree at the edge of the forest. Wilfred always wanted to play in the river, but both Caleb and Bamo refused to go anywhere near water. The river was *not* their friend.

Caleb began to behave well in school. He never got first in the class like Bamo. In fact, he struggled to get above #18, but he was no longer a problem to the teachers.

The chief let Caleb sleep over with Bamo all the time and he took both boys under his wing. He taught them bow hunting, which both boys were very good at. He told them all sorts of stories that at first seemed funny, but when they thought about them later, they realized Chief was teaching them lessons with his stories.

Jason and Stephanie also fell in love with Caleb. They spent extra hours tutoring him after school and encouraging him to be more serious about his education. They brought him books, but he didn't love them as much as Bamo did. He did appreciate the games and clothes though and wore them with pride.

The first time Jason saw Caleb play football, he said he had something special. For years, Jason had been bringing new footballs and jerseys for the kids in the village to play football with, but after he saw Caleb play, he brought him special fancy soccer shoes and an entire uniform. He bought him a huge poster of Didier Drogba, the most famous Ivorian football player. Jason hung the poster on the wall in Caleb's house and told him, "Every day you look at this poster and say, 'I'll be as great as Drogba one day!'"

As the boys got older, Jason kept talking about how Caleb's football skills could be his door to a better life. Bamo had been hearing that talk since he was little. His smarts would get him to a better life and now Caleb's football. He often wondered if this world Jason and Stephanie talked about was real.

Living in the chief's house, he had the best life of any child in the village. He ate meat several times a week. The house was the largest of any in the village. It had a huge parlor that it would take five of his mother's house to fill. It had meeting rooms for the chief and his staff. There were seven bedrooms in the house. Bamo had his own bedroom. No child in the whole village had a room of their own. It was actually too lonely for him. He was happiest when Caleb was spending the night.

The chief had a generator, so he actually had electricity in the house. And they didn't have to scrounge for water. There was always plenty supplied by the chief's different workers. Even the young boys in the village loved to bring water to the chief's house so he could bless them and think well of them and their families.

But this life Jason and Stephanie always spoke of was beyond his comprehension. Not only did they speak of it, but every book that Bamo read pointed to a different life. Detective mystery books were his favorite. He thought he would make a great detective because he was smart and could always figure out the story even before the end.

They brought magazines with pictures of people in clean, beautiful clothes living in places that looked like palaces and driving big, fancy cars. The houses were big with many rooms and the most beautiful furniture. The beds and chairs looked too beautiful to sleep or sit on. If Bamo had that kind of bed, he'd sleep on the floor just so the bed could stay beautiful.

Bamo had gotten to ride in the cars that Jason and Stephanie brought to the village when they came, but the cars in the magazines were sleek and shiny—not covered with mud, dents, and scratches.

Bamo loved his life in Oume. He loved living with Chief and Mama Gnale. He loved the fun he had every day with Caleb and Wilfred. He loved all the people in the village that had taken care of him, in spite of some of the difficulties he had encountered. But the more Jason talked to him about his future; the more he read books and found himself wanting to be inside the world he was reading about; the more he realized his teacher at school had taken him as far as she could take him and his head was longing for more knowledge...

Bamo began to think. He began to think more and more about how Stephanie told him that on the last trip before his mother died, she considered letting him go to America for high school instead of only for university. He began to think more and more about the room in their house Jason and Stephanie had promised him with his own nice bed and television. He thought about the education they promised, where he could get to study science and different kinds of math and could go into a building called a library that was completely filled with books.

He began to want that life they were telling him about. He began to want it so bad; it was all he could think about. He couldn't talk to anyone about it. It would seem as if he were ungrateful or unhappy for everything they had done for him in Oume. He couldn't bear Chief or Mama Gnale thinking that he wasn't happy living with them as a son. He couldn't bear to have Caleb think he wasn't the best friend.

Caleb dreamed of all the things they would do together as they grew older. Caleb loved farming and hunting and looked forward to a life where he lived off the land. He didn't understand Bamo's obsession with books and learning. He said they would marry on the same day in a joint ceremony under the Baobab tree. They would buy land right next to each other and farm together. They would raise their children together, and their daughters and sons would intermarry. They would be old men in the village together, well respected by all the youths.

Caleb had a smile on his face every time he told the story of their future. Bamo, instead, felt horrible dread in his stomach. Was it Jason and Stephanie's fault that he wasn't satisfied with the life God had given him? Was he supposed to be happy to grow old spending his whole life in Oume? Or was he supposed to be great and do great things in the world like Chief was always saying?

What did Chief mean that he was supposed to be great? What

did greatness really mean? Chief had been saying it for so many years, Bamo had begun to believe it.

One Saturday, Bamo was sitting in one of the main parlors in the chief's palace. For a few hours every Saturday afternoon, he had taken over his mother's role as the village reader. People brought him letters and documents and he'd help whoever needed him.

Chief Noumoury and Mama Gnale always looked on with pride when he did so. After a particularly long day of reading and writing for the people of the district villages, Bamo sat down to eat lunch with Chief Noumoury. As they were eating the roasted beef with tomato stew, Bamo asked the question that had been plaguing his heart.

"Is this what you mean by me being great? Me being able to help the people of the villages like my mother did?"

Bamo had gotten used to the chief's long pauses while he was thinking how best to answer a question.

He finally spoke. "It's a great thing you're doing for the people of the villages. A very great thing."

He sat quiet again. Bamo took another piece of beef and sopped up some of his sauce with it.

Chief spoke. "What you're called to, my son, is much greater than this. I've known it since you were a child."

He sat quietly for a moment, chewing his meat. Bamo wanted to ask him to please hurry and answer. This was not the time to be slow and thoughtful, measuring every word carefully to make sure the right amount of wisdom was being applied to the situation. Bamo stared at Chief. It felt like his whole future was sitting there on the tip of Chief's tongue. He finally swallowed the meat.

"Bamo, what do you think greatness is for you?"

Bamo wanted to shout. He didn't want Chief to ask him a long line of questions to lead him to his own truth. Sometimes when Chief Noumoury did that, it could be days later before Bamo figured out the wisdom hidden in the veiled phrases his father figure spoke. "Chief, I'm asking you the question because I don't know the answer. Please, can't you just tell me?"

"A man that has to be told his path to greatness is not worthy of it."

Bamo sat quiet, begging God to send him patience for the journey he knew Chief was about to take him on. "Yes, sir."

"There are many clues to a man's greatness, even when he is yet a child." Chief stirred his tomato sauce around on his rice. He signaled for the maid to refill his water.

"Look at the things you excel at and the things you love to do. Look at the things that come naturally to you and that your heart is given to. Look at the ways you help people and at the things you long to do to help people more. Look at what keeps you awake at night and what wakes you up in the morning. There is the key to your greatness."

Chief Noumoury ate his last piece of meat, took a large sip of water and signaled for the maid to clear his plate. Bamo sat thinking of everything he had said. He knew that any further questions would only lead Chief back to the things he had just said.

"Did you have enough to eat, son?"

"Yes, sir."

The chief clapped him on the back. As he stood from the table, he put his hand across Bamo's heart. "Your answers are all here, son. Don't look too far. Just search inside." He left to go meet his staff in his study.

Bamo sat at the table thinking for a few minutes, then went to his room. He wrote down all the things Chief Noumoury had said. He was no closer to getting an answer than he was when he asked his first question, but he had something to think about.

Two months later, Jason and Stephanie came to Oume for one of their regular visits. As always, they stayed in the Chief's palace in a room down the hall from Bamo. The first night after they arrived, Bamo was awake all night, reading one of the new detective books Jason brought him. Bamo's English had gotten so good, he served as Jason's translator everywhere they went. They had a meeting with the chief and his staff about reviving Diaka's plans to build a school in the village.

Bamo skipped his school in town the whole two weeks they were there to help them at Diaka's little school building in the village. His mother's young friend, Aunty Aicha, had kept the school going all those years, glad to carry on her legacy. Bamo enjoyed teaching the young kids of the village. He loved giving them knowledge and gave them little speeches every day on the importance of education. He felt his mother smiling from heaven the whole time he was in her school.

He went with Jason, Stephanie and the chief to the district village meetings to discuss how to bring a consistent supply of clean water to the villages. Chief was always taking Bamo to meetings with him, saying he was training him how to be a great man. Bamo sat bored most of the time. But these meetings were different. He liked thinking about ways to make the lives of the people—his people—better.

A couple of times, he had to remind himself he was only there to translate. He was still a child. No one was asking for his opinion. But then they did. And he spoke. And the district leaders nodded and smiled, impressed by the wisdom of a youth.

He and Jason went on long walks, discussing his future. Bamo asked as many questions as his still growing English would allow. Jason answered every one and each time he answered, the desire in Bamo's heart expanded all the more. They stood under the Baobab tree late one evening, and after answering all his questions, Jason asked him a question that made Bamo's heart race.

"Bamo, did you know your mother was in agreement that you should be educated in the US?"

Bamo nodded, not trusting his voice to speak.

"We didn't agree on when, but she did consent for you to come."

Bamo nodded again, hoping that Jason was leading to the place he hoped with this conversation.

"Have you thought about it? When you would like to come?"

Bamo shrugged.

Jason laughed and clapped him on the back. "My friend, if I could take you back on the plane with me, I would. You let me know when you're ready."

Bamo could barely lift his legs to go back to the chief's house. Was this the time for him to go to America?

Two days before Jason and Stephanie were to leave, Bamo was awake the whole night thinking. The next morning at breakfast, he could hardly eat.

"What's wrong, Bamo? You don't like your rice pudding? Do you want more bread?" Mama Gnale asked.

"No, Mama. I'm fine."

"But you're not eating. Are you sick?"

"No, Mama. I'm fine. I'm not sick at all."

She sat there watching him for a second. Bamo knew he should force himself to finish his pudding, but he couldn't.

The whole night he was thinking about how much he loved reading books and learning. He loved teaching the children in the school. He loved meeting with other leaders to see how they could improve the lives of the people in the village. He thought about Jason's question about when he wanted to come to America.

"Bamo, I can have the cook fry you some *alloko*. Do you want the leftover spinach soup from last night?"

"Gnale, leave Bamo. He's fine."

Bamo looked up at the chief. The chief looked him straight in the eyes. "My son, have you discovered your path to greatness?"

Bamo sat quiet for a second. He looked down at his plate. He took a deep breath and looked back up at the chief. "Yes, father. I have."

"Are you ready to walk that path?"

Bamo nodded. "Yes, father. I am."

"Okay then." He took a bite of rice pudding and followed it with some bread. He sipped his tea and then turned to Jason and then looked at Stephanie. "It's time. Bamo may travel to America to be with you people and to go to that school you've spoken of."

Stephanie's mouth flew open. "Really?" She quickly translated the chief's words for Jason.

Jason's face broke into a big smile. "Really, sir? Wow!"

Jason looked at Bamo. "You're ready? To go now?"

Bamo nodded and laughed. The knot that had been churning in his stomach the last few days melted. "Yes, Mr. Jason. I'm ready. I'm so ready."

A few tears streamed down Mama Gnale's face. "Bamo, you want to leave your mother?"

"Gnale, leave Bamo. It's time for him to follow the path God has for him. He doesn't *want* to leave you. He *has* to leave you." Chief looked at Bamo. "At least for now. But your son will return, and he will be a great gift to this village."

Bamo nodded. "Yes, father. I will."

Chapter 11

⟨⁓∞⁓⟩

The next few months flew by in a confusing blur trips to town to make pictures and documents. Chief taking trips to Abidjan, and finally Bamo traveling to Abidjan for the first time to go to the embassy. The city of his mother's birth was big and crowded, full of cars with blaring horns and many people yelling at each other. But it also had a feeling so different from the village.

He and Chief stayed at Aunt Namassa's house. She had continued to visit Bamo over the years, but he hadn't seen his uncles since his mother's funeral. He asked Aunt Namassa why, but she pressed her lips together and shook her head. Bamo knew better than to ask a second time.

Bamo remembered the moment where Chief arose with a quiet happiness and announced to him, "Our God has done it. Your papers have been approved in a very fast time. I will call Stephanie and Jason. It's time for you to go, my son. God has done it."

Bamo felt fear and excitement at the same time. Ever since he accepted to travel to America for school, he had mixed feelings. He hoped life there would be everything he hoped. But then he knew that many people that tried to travel never got papers, so he tried to not think about everything that was happening so he wouldn't get disappointed.

After they called Jason and Stephanie, his plane ticket was bought. They told him to give away all his things and that he would get new clothes and shoes when he arrived. The village held the biggest celebration for him under the Baobab tree and people came from all the district villages. The people loved him as they had loved his mother Diaka, and they came out in droves to see him off. All his teachers from the school in town came, so did the people he read letters for; in fact, the people were more than he had ever seen in the clearing.

The food was so much and Bamo was glad that the people were getting to eat on his behalf. Chief Noumoury had ordered food to be brought out from the village store.

The celebration lasted for hours and it felt like Bamo greeted each person individually. The kids shook his hand in admiration and begged him not to forget them. The mothers and fathers laid their hand on his head and blessed him, his journey, and his future.

Mama Gnale cried throughout the whole celebration, as did Aunty Aicha, his mother's friend. Caleb had been distant since Bamo first told him he was going to America. He kept his distance the whole day at the celebration. He was there but didn't say more than two words to Bamo or anyone else.

After people had returned to the other villages and their homes, Chief Noumoury walked with Bamo back to the house. It was as if the older man wanted to share the wisdom of all his years with Bamo in that walk from the Baobab tree to the palace. Bamo wished he could capture every word and hold them in his heart. Oh, how we would miss his chief father. Mr. Jason was nice and was a very good man, but no one had loved and cared for him as the chief had.

Even though he didn't say a word, Caleb followed them to the chief's house and sat in the parlor. He glanced at Bamo every few minutes but continued his sulking. Just as Bamo was about to go beg him not to be upset, Aunty Aicha was led into the parlor by the chief's house steward.

She came to Bamo with tears in her eyes. She had a small brown wallet in her hands. It looked worn and dirty, like it was old and about to fall apart at any moment. "Bamo, I have something for you." She looked around and led him to a chair across the room from where Caleb was sulking. Whatever she needed to share seemed to be private.

She opened the brown wallet and pulled out something shiny. She rubbed it on her shirt and indicated for Bamo to hold out his hands. "This is from your mother. She gave it to me the day she died. Quite by accident actually, but we know there are no accidents. She said it has been in your family for more than a hundred years and is given to the oldest child in the family. It's yours now, Bamo."

Bamo's eyes filled with tears to match Aunty Aicha's. "My mother?"

She nodded.

He studied the gold necklace. His tears flowed freely as Aunty Aicha explained the bull and the lion. She closed Bamo's hands around the chain. "You take very good care of this gift from your mother. And when you're older, you'll give it to your first child."

Bamo put the chain around his neck. He would put it into the wallet Jason and Stephanie had given him before he slept, but for now, he wanted to feel his mother's gift close to his skin. Aunty Aicha pressed the old brown wallet into his hands. He smiled. She understood that he would want to keep anything that had belonged to his mother.

After she left, Bamo went over to where Caleb was sitting. "Come on, my brother. I'm leaving tomorrow. Do you really want to spend our last few hours together being mad?"

Tears started spilling down Caleb's face as he shook his head.

"Come on." Bamo indicated for Caleb to follow him to his room. When they got there, Bamo took an old oil drum filled with coins he had been collecting since he was a child. "This is all my money. It's for you to go to town every week and use the Internet so you can write me.

Caleb nodded and a little smile appeared as he wiped his face with the back of his hand. He had complained on the many trips when Bamo forced him to go to town to learn to use the Internet. Bamo was glad he didn't let up on him.

Bamo stretched out his arms. "Everything in this room belongs to you now. You can keep it, give it away, burn it, whatever you want to do. Everything is yours."

Bamo had already given his entire book collection to the school in town. Caleb's mouth fell open. Bamo laughed and grabbed his friend. They hugged and cried for a long time. Bamo looked his friend in the eye. "I'm going, but I will be back. And I promise everything I do in America is for me and you. We probably will grow old together in this village, but it'll be a much better place because of me leaving. Do you understand?"

Caleb nodded. The friends stayed up all night talking. Bamo knew he had a long day ahead of him the next day, but it would be worth being tired just to have those hours talking to his best friend.

Chapter 12

On the day of departure, early in the morning, a special traditional gathering was held for Bamo's departure called the blessing ceremony. It was always done in Oume when someone was leaving for a long period or when their return was unsure. Early that morning, the drummer announced the beginning of the ceremony and the people of Oume and the surrounding villages all gathered at the Baobab tree. Chief Noumoury and Gnale stood with their staff behind them. Bamo stood facing them, arm's distance away.

With a look of love and pride on his face, Chief Noumoury extended his right arm and put it on Bamo's left shoulder. Behind Bamo stood a long line of villagers—all the fathers he had lived with at the beginning. The first father in line extended his right arm and put it on Bamo's left shoulder, underneath the chief's hand. The men of the village lined up behind that first father, all standing in support of Bamo.

Mama Gnale extended her arm and put it on Bamo's right shoulder. The women of the village, starting with Bamo's mothers, stood behind him. His first mother put her hand on his right shoulder, under Mama Gnale's hand, and all the women of the village stood behind her.

Once everyone was properly aligned, Chief Noumoury began praying over Bamo with the entire group of mothers and fathers praying silently in agreement. Chief prayed that God would protect Bamo on his journey and that He would bring Bamo safely home at the appointed time.

Tears were streaming down the faces of many during the prayer. After the ceremony, the entire population lined up to hug and bless Bamo before he departed for the airport.

Mama Gnale cried the entire trip from Oume to Abidjan and then from Aunt Namassa's house to the airport and then entire time in the airport until they had dropped him off at the very last place people without tickets to travel could go.

Aunty Namassa seemed fine from her house to the airport. But then when she hugged him in the airport, she saw his mother's necklace around his neck. She fingered it, turned it over and stared at it, and then her tears started flowing. She kept saying how proud his mother would have been to see where he was going in life.

Chief hardly talked the whole time. Every time he started to share what Bamo knew would have been wise words, it seemed like they got caught in his throat. He stopped talking, patted Bamo on the back and looked away.

Bamo cried in the airport as he waved goodbye to Chief Noumoury and his two heads of staff who had traveled with them, Mama Gnale and Aunt Namassa, Uncle Solo and her children. They made a big show in the airport with their goodbyes, but nobody paid much attention because they were saying goodbyes of their own.

Bamo saw a couple of other young people like him, crying and being cried over by a huge group of family members. There were older people saying goodbye to families who must have traveled more often because there were less tears. And then there were the people that looked like they traveled all the time, looking somewhat annoyed and impatient as they pushed through the piles of first time travelers and their families to get to wherever they were going in such a hurry.

Finally, Chief pulled him to the side and managed to get some words out. "Bamo, I am very proud of you. I'm happy for what

God has done for your life. I am happy that you're going after the dreams of your heart." His voice caught.

"As you go through that door to get on the plane, I don't want you to look back. You hear me? There will be days that you will be lonely, and you will want to run home to the life you've known in Oume. Block that thought out of your heart."

Bamo observed the knot in his throat rise and fall from emotion. His own feelings were making his head spin as a football in the air.

Chief continued, "You're going to stay. You hear me? You know that you're always welcome in Oume and in my home, but today I'm telling you, don't come back home until you've finished your course. Don't come back until you've done all you're supposed to do."

Bamo gulped. The finality of getting on that plane was becoming real to him. He couldn't imagine not being in Oume. "What about when Jason and Stephanie come to visit?"

Chief gave him a look. "Son, stay until you finish your path. You'll know when that is. You'll feel it in your soul. Oume will call you and it will be time to come home. That's when you come. You understand?"

Bamo nodded with tears streaming down his face. Chief pulled him into an embrace.

"I love you, son. Son of Diaka. Son of Oume." His voice broke. "Son of Chief Noumoury." Bamo cried for a few minutes in his arms until Chief finally clapped him on the back and pushed him away.

The whole day was overwhelming and confusing and after many hugs and pats on the back from his family, he was all alone. They went as far as they could and then they couldn't go any further. And then Bamo was on his own. Headed to a new world and a new life. He was excited but scared.

If the airport was any indication of the life he was headed to, he had a lot to learn. His stomach was nervous, so he had to keep going to the bathroom. The toilet was confusing. There was a white bowl hanging on the wall and men would stand in front of it and then when they were finished, they pushed a handle and water poured into the toilet.

Then there were little rooms with a door with a big bowl on a stand on the floor. He wasn't sure what happened in those rooms because the doors were closed when men went inside.

Because his stomach was so nervous, Bamo had to poo, but when he went to sit on the little bowl against the wall, another man yelled at him and called him a village boy and pointed for him to go inside a little room with the bowl on the stand to take care of his business.

When he finished, he couldn't figure out a way to make the water come rushing in to make his poo go away. He panicked because it would make him look like a village boy to leave his poo in the toilet and he didn't want anyone else to yell at him about being a village boy.

He stayed in the little room until he didn't hear anybody else in the bathroom, and then he ran out of the stall. He washed his hands like he had seen other people do and then left the bathroom as quickly as possible.

The airport was confusing, so Bamo was happy they had assigned a person to stay with him to get him to the plane. It felt like it took forever, but they finally escorted him to the big door that would put him on the plane to America.

Bamo felt even more alone when the person that had been taking him everywhere in the airport said her goodbyes and left him on the plane. He was seated next to an older woman, smartly dressed in a fancy outfit with glasses and fancy braids in her hair. Something about her made her look like she traveled all the time. Bamo hoped she was nice.

He was sitting in a chair next to the path where people were walking, and the woman was sitting next to the window. Bamo wanted to sit next to the window, but then again, he was scared of what he might see. Some people told him that flying would make him closer to God and the angels. If he sat next to the window, would he see God?

The woman next to him pushed a few buttons on a grey screen on the back of the chair in front of her. Bamo was surprised when it lit up with pictures. She kept pushing buttons until a picture show started playing. Bamo didn't realize he was leaning over into her seat so he could see until she laughed and took out the little circle things she had stuck in her ears.

She said something to him, but he didn't understand. He asked as politely as he could, "Excuse me? I didn't understand."

She looked shocked. "You speak English?"

He nodded, proud that he could communicate with this woman who looked so smart and rich.

"Is this your first time flying? And where did you learn English?"

The woman looked interested while he told her the story of Jason and Stephanie coming to Oume and bringing him to America. He kept getting interrupted by somebody making announcements in English and French about how to prepare for the flight.

After a few minutes, the woman dressed in a uniform who had introduced herself as the air hostess who would be taking care of him came and fastened a belt around his waist. Talking to the woman in the seat next to him, who had introduced herself as Eva, almost made him forget he was about to fly. When the air hostess strapped the belt around him, fear gripped him.

Eva laughed and said, "Don't worry, Bamo. Flying is very safe. Safer than driving. You'll be fine." She patted him on the arm.

Since he could speak English and was neatly dressed in a shirt and tie his Aunt Namassa had brought him from the big market in Abidjan, Eva probably didn't realize that Bamo had hardly ever been in a car. Let alone an airplane.

As panic started to fill his heart, he saw two little boys, running up and down the aisles playing. They weren't the least bit afraid of flying. If children could feel safe, then certainly he should. And God was going to take care of him anyway.

Soon it was time for the plane to take off. Even though he had gone to the bathroom right before getting on the flight, Bamo was sure he'd pee his pants. His ears were making funny clicking feelings, and his stomach dropped to his feet. He must have looked terrified because Eva laughed and took his hand. She held it until they no longer felt like they were pointing upward.

She leaned back so he could look out the window. The ground below got smaller and smaller until it disappeared. He could see clouds. He closed his eyes, sure that if he kept looking, he would see God. He sat with his eyes closed for a while, thanking God for the opportunity to go to America and praying that the plane would stay in the air until they got to America.

After a while, the air hostesses came by with a cart and asked if he would like to drink something. Bamo didn't want to drink anything. The person announcing things on the plane said that they would be flying for eight hours. If he drank something, he would have to go to the bathroom, and he didn't think he could hold it until they landed.

They came by with food. When he refused again, the air hostess insisted that he eat. "But what if I have to go the bathroom?" He thought about it. Everybody on the plane was eating and drinking. What would they all do?

The air hostess laughed. "We have a bathroom in the back. When you need to go, you just tell me and I'll take you."

Bamo nodded, eyes wide in wonder. There was a bathroom on the plane? He couldn't even begin to think of how that would work.

"Do you want fish or chicken?"

Bamo bowed his head. "I don't have any money for food." He did have some small money Chief had given him, but he wanted to save it for an emergency. He could go awhile without eating.

Eva and the air hostess laughed together. Eva patted his arm. "You don't have to pay for the food, Bamo. Please eat, dear."

Bamo smiled. "Okay, give me the best one."

The stewardess laughed. She put a small tray in front of him. It had little plastic containers of food. There was bread and a cake and some type of salad and then a hot dish with meat and sauce and rice. He started eating with his hands, but Eva clucked at him.

"Bamo, you'll use your cutlery! You can't eat with your hands anymore dear, okay? Where you're going, you have to learn to use them."

Bamo stared at the cutlery for a second. Eva shook her head and showed him each one and how to use it and what to use it for. It was awkward. Bamo kept dropping food, but eventually he got through the meal. Would Jason and Stephanie insist that he use cutlery, too? They ate with their hands like everybody else in the village. But they probably didn't do that in America.

Bamo looked over at Eva. He wanted to ask her everything he would need to know for his new home in America. She could give him a quick lesson in proper eating, how to flush the toilet and...he didn't even know what else he didn't know. But Eva was watching her movie. He didn't want to bother her anymore.

When the stewardess came to clear his food tray, she brought him headphones and showed him how to use the television on the back of the chair in front of him.

Bamo usually fell asleep after eating, and he was really sleepy since he had been up all night with Caleb the night before, but he was completely mesmerized by the television screen and the pictures and the people and the stories that played across it. It was like watching a book! He thought of all the books he'd read over the years that Jason and Stephanie had brought them. He wondered if they had movies for each book.

All the air hostesses kept coming to check on him, bringing snacks and drinks and helping him choose new movies. They showed him how to use the tiny toilet in the tiny room that he could barely move around in. He was up watching movies and eating when he heard them announcing it was time for breakfast.

Breakfast? Had he stayed awake the whole night? Maybe he should try to sleep quickly so he would be fine by the time he reached Jason and Stephanie. He wanted to be on his toes in his new world–knowing how to flush the toilet and eat with cutlery and whatever else he would be expected to do.

No matter how hard he tried, he couldn't sleep. Too many thoughts were rushing through his head. Questions, fears, excitement, anticipation... and one question rang the loudest as they flew further and further away from the only home he had ever known.

Had he made the right decision?

A little while later, the captain made the announcement that they were making their descent into Paris. Bamo panicked.

"Paris!" he shouted. "I'm not going to Paris. I'm supposed to be going to America. Oh, no!" He pushed the call button the air hostess had told him to push if he needed something.

He hadn't touched it the whole flight. The air hostesses were working hard enough. He didn't want to trouble them. Plus, before he could think of wanting anything, they were already there, bringing him things he didn't ask for. Extra blankets because he had never experienced that kind of cold air. Pillows, headphones, snacks, magazines with pictures of places all over the world.

The air hostess hurried over to him. "What's wrong, Bamo?"

He began crying. "They put me on the wrong plane. I'm supposed to be going to America. Not Paris."

She laughed and patted his arm. "Calm down, Bamo. America is a long way away, so we have to go to Paris first. You'll go to a different plane. That one will take you to America. Okay?"

Bamo nodded and sniffled.

"Is your seatbelt fastened? We're going to land soon."

She buckled it for him and pulled it tighter around his waist. As she walked away, he grabbed her arm and said, "Wait, how do we land?"

She smiled and leaned over his seat. Using her hands, she showed him how the plane would come down out of the air and touch down on the ground. "You'll only feel a little bump. Okay? It's very safe."

Bamo wasn't sure about it. What if they just fell out of the sky?

"Bamo, trust me, I've been flying all over the world for ten years. And I've never had one bad landing. Relax, okay? I'll be back to get you once we've landed."

Bamo nodded.

Eva woke up just in time to hold his hand, just as she had when they were taking off. The landing went exactly as the air hostess described. He watched out the window as they got closer and closer to the ground, and then he felt a little bump. People started clapping.

He screamed out loud, "God is powerful! I am on the ground!"

Everyone in the plane started laughing.

Eva said her goodbyes before rushing off to another flight and Bamo waited for the air hostess to take him to the plane to America.

The airport in Paris was so big. Bamo had never seen anything like it. There were big stores with big pictures in the windows of white people in funny looking clothes. Some of the pictures had a man and a woman together and Bamo had to close his eyes because it seemed like they were doing private things that shouldn't be plastered on a big window for all to see.

There were stores with food everywhere. Bamo had eaten so much on the plane that he didn't think of eating another bite. People had told him that people that travel to America always get fat and he could see why. There was so much food. It made him a little sad. People in his country were starving and yet everywhere he turned there was so much food.

The air hostess turned him over to another attendant and the young woman was nice enough to let Bamo walk around everywhere. In and out of every store. He stopped and stared at every restaurant. They were even places where the floor moved and carried you while you stood still. There were stairs that moved for you while you stood still, too. The attendant took him on an elevator. He didn't like it when the doors closed and the box began to move, and it felt like his stomach went down to his feet.

To get to his plane, they had to ride a bus. Everything was big and colorful and rich looking and the whole world was moving too fast.

And there were white people everywhere. Bamo knew that he would see mostly white people when he left Africa, but he didn't know what it would feel like to look into pale, white faces everywhere he turned. He was used to Jason and Stephanie, so he wasn't surprised by the stringy hair, thin noses and lines for lips. But they were everywhere–so many of them. He would have never imagined anything like it where he was from.

By the time he got to his plane to America, Bamo was completely exhausted. As soon as the air hostess strapped him into his seatbelt, he fell asleep. He slept through all the movies and all the meals and only stirred when he felt the plane bump onto the ground.

When the captain announced that they had landed safely in Atlanta, Bamo's heart pounded in his chest. Would Jason and Stephanie be there waiting for him? What was America like? He had already seen so much in Paris that was different than anything he ever dreamed of, no matter how many books he had read.

Would he be able to handle life in America?

Chapter 13

Bamo was glad he slept the entire flight because when he got off the plane in Atlanta, it seemed like the whole world was moving fast. People were almost running and pushing past one another. He and the attendant that met him at the plane had to take a train to get to where Jason and Stephanie would be waiting for him.

Bamo had never been on a train before. He would have liked it better if he could have gotten a seat and if the people weren't pushing. A white man scowled at him when the train took off too fast and Bamo fell over his bag. "Hold on!"

Bamo wondered if everybody in Atlanta would be so mean. Jason and Stephanie were nice, so he hoped most of the people were like them.

When they got off the train, they had to take a huge moving staircase up. At the top were beautiful pictures. There was a young, black girl smiling on the picture with her arms open wide. Bamo felt like she was welcoming him to America. He smiled back at her. When he got to the top of the moving stairs, he heard his name being screamed.

"Bamo, over here!"

He didn't even have time to worry about whether Jason and Stephanie would be there waiting for him. They were right there at the top of the stairs with a big white sign with his name on it.

Bamo looked at the attendant to make sure it was okay to go. As soon as he got the okay, he took off in a run straight into Jason's arms. Jason and Stephanie hugged him together. When they finished, Stephanie's face was red, and she had tears in her eyes.

"We're so happy you're here. I can't believe it's finally happened after all these years. You're here with us." Stephanie hugged him again.

Bamo lost himself in that hug. All of his fears from the whole time of traveling dissolved in her arms. He had done the right thing. He was going to be okay. More than okay. He was on his way to becoming the great man his father chief said he was going to be.

"That's enough, Stephanie." Jason clapped Bamo on the back. "Come on, Buddy. Let's get you home. You must be tired."

Bamo nodded. He was too overwhelmed to speak.

Jason and Stephanie had told him to leave everything in Oume, so Bamo only had a backpack with a few of his favorite books he didn't want to leave behind, a shirt Caleb had given him to remember him by, and his mother's favorite dress. There was no way he was leaving that behind. It and the necklace were the only things he had left of hers.

⚬⚯⚬

Bamo had spent the last hour with his mouth open, eyes wide, unable to speak more than a few words in acknowledgement of everything Jason and Stephanie were showing him. They had taken him into a large hall full of cars. Bamo had never seen so many cars in his life. They took him to their car, which was like a pickup truck, but the back was closed with seats. They drove on a busy highway filled with many cars.

They finally arrived at their house after a while. Their neighborhood was filled with big houses. Bamo had never seen anything so big in his life. They pulled their truck into a room inside the house.

Stephanie sang out, "Welcome home, Bamo!"

The house was so big; he wondered how many other families they would live with there. He hoped that whoever else lived with them was just as excited about his coming. Chief's house was big, but that was because he was a chief. Bamo wondered if Jason was chief of this neighborhood, but then he realized all the houses were big.

Bamo shook off his confusion as they led him into the house.

At home in their living room, they immediately called Aunt Namassa's neighbor who ran down the stretch to fetch her.

When Aunt Namassa heard his voice, she started to cry for joy.

Bamo cried with her and said, "Aunty, I am in America. I have reached. I will work hard to send you everything I can."

"Bamo, you're not there to work. You're there for school. Don't worry about us. God is taking care of us."

"Aunty, please send a message to the village that I am well in America and I want to thank everyone for their prayers."

They talked for about five more minutes. "Bamo, you respect Jason and Stephanie, their friends, relatives and neighbors and everybody there in America. I know you'll make us proud, my son."

After he hung up with his aunt. Jason and Stephanie took him around their big house. There was a big kitchen, a big room with a big dining table, another big room with a big television and big couches. Upstairs there were four bedrooms, all big. Americans lived like they were giants. One of the bedrooms was Jason and Stephanie's and the other had a desk and other things for an office, so Bamo realized no other families lived with them. This whole house was just for the three of them.

When they got to his room, Bamo's mouth dropped open again. He looked at Jason and Stephanie with huge eyes and they laughed and nodded. It was decorated with his name on the wall, pictures of him in Oume and a big picture of him and his mother. Bamo teared up when he saw it.

Jason was always snapping pictures in the village, but Bamo

didn't know he had saved them. He didn't know he could make them big and put them on the wall. There was a picture of him with Daddy Chief and Mama Gnale and another picture of him and his best bro, Caleb.

Bamo hugged Jason and Stephanie and thanked them for the pictures. They would make sure he never got too homesick for Oume.

He had a big bed with lots of big, fluffy pillows. Just as they promised, he had a television of his own.

"This is...my...this is for me?" Bamo stammered.

Jason put his hands on his shoulders. "All yours. We have to come up with a schedule for the television though. Only certain hours. We don't want it to interrupt your studies."

"No, Mr. Jason. It could never interrupt my studies. Nothing is more important than that."

"Bamo, you don't have to call me Mr. Jason. Just call me Jason. Okay?"

Bamo's eyes flew open. He shook his head. "I can't do that." He shook his head even more vigorously. Call a grown-up by their first name? He could never.

Jason and Stephanie laughed.

"Are you ready to eat?"

Bamo nodded. He had slept the entire way on the plane, so he hadn't eaten since the attendant bought him something in Paris.

"Okay, you can shower while I go put the food on the table," Stephanie said.

Jason showed him to his bathroom. His own bathroom. Bamo couldn't believe he had a whole bathroom to himself. Mr. Jason gave him a towel and some soap.

Probably because he stayed in Bamo's village so many times over the years, he realized he needed to explain how everything worked. He showed Bamo how to work the toilet, sink and shower and how to make sure the water was the right temperature. Jason laughed when Bamo asked him how they made the water flow hot from the tap.

Bamo took his first hot shower. It felt like warm rain falling from heaven. He knew he had stayed in there too long when the whole bathroom filled with fog. He couldn't even see himself in the mirror.

Bamo wiped the mirror with the thick, fuzzy towel Jason had given him. It would be funny to look at himself every day. He grinned and waved at himself. He stared for a minute. Was he handsome? In all the books he read, they always talked about whether a man was handsome or a woman was beautiful. He would have to ask Jason and Stephanie how his own looks would be rated.

Jason had showed him a chest and a closet full of clothes all his size. Even though they sent and brought him clothes in Oume every year, this was over the top. He had five pairs of jeans, three pairs of "khakis" as Jason had called them, and a couple of "dress pants" for church. Bamo stopped counting his shirts when he got to twenty. Why would one boy need twenty shirts? He had three pairs of sports shoes. Three. He could only wear one at a time. There were some fancier shoes that Bamo was sure he was supposed to wear with the dress pants for church. There were a couple of shoes like the ones they used to send/bring to Oume for him to wear.

There was a whole drawer of socks and underwear. A whole drawer. Why did Jason and Stephanie think he needed so much?

Bamo put on a pair of jeans and a t-shirt that read, "American Eagle." It had the American flag on it and Bamo wondered if they had it especially made for his arrival.

Stephanie called them down to the dining room. Bamo's mouth dropped open yet again at the huge spread of food on the table.

"Can I take some and send it to my friends and family members at home?"

Jason and Stephanie laughed. Jason said, "Buddy, it would spoil before it gets there."

Bamo couldn't stop staring. Why did they need so much food for three people? This food could feed fifty people for a whole day.

Jason prayed over the food.

When he finished, Bamo said his own prayer. "Dear God, thank you for bringing me to paradise. Please, take care of my people for me—my mothers, brothers, sisters, fathers and everyone in the village for me. Give me the strength to help them. God make the farms productive and make the harvest produce enough food for everyone including surrounding villages. Help me to succeed. It is my promise to you, God, that if You help me knowing what I have been through, that I will help my village and all other villages if You give me the means. Thank you so very much for Jason and Stephanie for doing all they did for Oume, just in the name of love. Please watch over them, secure them financially and healthwise to accomplish all their dreams. Thank you, God."

Jason and Stephanie paused for a moment, both looking at him with love in their eyes.

Bamo rubbed his hands together. "Okay, let's eat!"

Chapter 14

Just as he had for his last six years in America, Bamo woke up with the sun. It was a habit from his days in Oume village that he had never shaken.

Adjusting to life in America had been difficult at first. The fast pace, the extravagance and waste, the way people didn't seem to care for each other very much and didn't even bother to greet their neighbors every day. Everything went too fast and people were too busy. He never really understood why. What was so important that made them go so fast? Didn't they understand how lovely it was just to sit still, to talk to someone for hours without hurrying off to the next thing?

Junior high and high school had been good for him. He thanked God every day for his good life with Jason and Stephanie in Clarkston, a suburb outside of Atlanta that had a lot of immigrants from a lot of different countries. Bamo had gone to school with kids from many different nations. It kept him from feeling completely homesick, and he was able to get to know different cultures, foods, and ways of life. But now he wasn't in his nice bedroom in Clarkston anymore. He was in a dorm room at Emory University where he had a full scholarship in International Studies and Development.

Living in America had made him realize how poor his people in Oume were. How they didn't have so many of the necessities that were normal here in America. The more he lived his life in America and the more he received letters about how hard life continued

112

to be back in Oume, he was more and more committed to bringing change. Everything he did in America was for the purpose of improving the lives of his family back in Oume and other villages in his country. This degree was just a part of that plan.

Bamo got out of bed and got dressed for his morning run. He had started running in the mornings since he had come to University. Atlanta wasn't like Oume, where one walked everywhere they went, often many kilometers every day. In America, one could go weeks without walking very far at all. During junior and high school, Bamo had insisted on walking to school every day, even though Jason offered to drop him off on his way to work.

When he got to University though, he lived on campus. The walk to his classes wasn't enough. Plus, he was no longer eating Stephanie's well-cooked meals. He was eating college food, which included too many burgers and fries and pizza. At the end of his first year of University, he felt thick and slow. He knew he had a problem when Jason had to take him shopping for new jeans and khakis. The ones they had bought for the school year had gotten too tight.

When Stephanie grabbed a thick piece of flesh that had somehow grown around his middle, he knew he had to take matters into his own hands. He took up running. He loved to go at 5:30 am, when the air was cool and crisp. Every morning, the sun greeted him by splaying beautiful colors across the sky. Sunrise was nowhere near as beautiful as it was in Oume. There were too many buildings that blocked his view of the vast sky he was used to in his little village.

After his run, he took a long, hot shower. It was one of his main indulgences in the last six years. Stephanie used to fuss at him about using up all the hot water in the house, but Jason always told her to let him be.

He didn't have classes but he had a meeting with his study group. He took extra care to iron creases in the cotton shirt he wore. Normally, he would just throw on some jeans and a t-shirt, but for some reason, he was ironing a white shirt and khakis to wear. Putting the creases in almost made him late, and Bamo hated being late.

His study group was made up of people from many different countries—China, India, Kenya, Cameroon, Nigeria, and a few from the US. They studied together often and once a month had a gathering where everyone brought food from their country. It was always a good time, and they had become like a family to Bamo.

Bamo checked his watch just as he was running into the study room in the library where his group met. He was only five minutes late. Some of his Nigerian friends still showed up more than thirty minutes late. A few of them had straightened out after they were told they wouldn't be a part of the group, but there were two—Femi and Chuks who couldn't seem to be on time no matter what. They always joked, "white man made watches, but black man keeps time."

Everyone cheered his name when he walked in. Their greeting always warmed his heart. Bamo looked for a seat.

"Over here, Bamo." Krystal patted the seat next to her.

Bamo gulped. He looked around the room, but every seat was full. Femi and Chuks would have to drag chairs in when they arrived.

"Hi, Krystal." Bamo swallowed again. His mouth seemed to go dry whenever he was around her. She was a very nice girl, and he had spent more time with her than anyone in their study group.

She had invited him to go with her to help out at a feeding program for the homeless in Midtown Atlanta. It unsettled him that day to be so close to poor and hungry people in America. He realized that Jason and Stephanie had kept him pretty sheltered in Clarkston.

He didn't understand how people could be poor in a country like America. There were opportunities everywhere. Even he had been able to work at the little grocery store in their neighborhood his last few years of high school. That was a battle he'd had to fight with Jason and Stephanie. They had treated him so well and took care of his every need, but he wanted to be able to make his own spending money and be able to send money home to Oume, no matter how small.

"Hey, Bamo." She smiled that big, cheery smile of hers and touched his arm. Her smile and her fingers were warm, and it gave Bamo a funny feeling in his chest.

He'd had that same feeling in his chest while watching her serve at the homeless shelter. She touched and hugged the homeless women and their children and was sweet and cheery, as she always was.

She didn't act like many of the black American girls he had met. He couldn't seem to understand them and their long, fake hair and nails and heavy makeup. He felt like some of them treated him funny when they found out he was African. Even though he'd had the best marks in all his years of school, they still seemed to try to make him feel small. Not all of them. There were others who were warm and kind and asked him funny questions about his life in Africa.

"I brought you something." Krystal turned to reach into her bag. She pulled out a tin. Bamo knew that inside were his favorite brownies that Krystal baked for him a couple times a month since the first time he had tasted them at one of their study group dinners.

His eyes grew big. "Krystal, you want to make me fat again?"

She laughed. "You're hardly fat." She poked him in the side. "You could stand to put on a few pounds, Bamo. You should stop running so much and eat more."

Bamo blushed. Somehow, she reminded him of his mother when she said that. He had very few memories of his mother, but she always complained that he ran too much and didn't eat enough. Mama Gnale used to say the same thing.

He turned to listen to their study group leader, Feng. Feng was from China and was a very intense fellow who always felt the need to keep the group focused when they talked and laughed too much.

They broke into groups based on their different subjects to

study for their upcoming exams. Krystal was in the same group. She had the same major, so they had many classes together.

When Bamo had asked her why she was interested in International Development, Krystal had explained that her parents were missionaries and she had grown up in Haiti and then Panama. She had only lived in America when she started college. He knew that's what made her different. She had grown up in environments not too different from his village in Oume, and like him, she wanted to come up with solutions to help and bring lasting change.

She had lived for many years in Haiti and then had studied French her first two years at Emory, so they spoke in French to each other all the time. She was very dark-skinned with natural hair and could have easily passed for a woman from his country. When they had long conversations in French, she made him feel like he was talking to someone from home.

She was passionate and outspoken, and Bamo always found himself drawn to the words she spoke. Her words sounded like music. Krystal liked to write poetry and when she spoke, it came out in poems.

Bamo's study group went to a separate room next to the big meeting room where they all initially gathered. They had comfortable chairs and a big table and a white board with erasable markers on the board.

"So, what shall we do for this final project?" Feng asked in a quiet, serious voice.

"Final project? Shouldn't we be focusing on exams first? The project isn't due for another three months," Indira, a student from India said.

Bamo thought her tone was a little sharper than it needed to be. It always was. She had an air about her like she thought she was better than everyone. Her parents had a lot of money and she always acted like the rest of them were poor and desperate. When it was her turn to host their monthly dinner, she'd had a lavishly catered event at her parents' large house in Buckhead. But to Bamo, it wasn't because she wanted to treat them well, it was because she wanted to show off. He could feel it.

Feng remained calm. "It's not good to wait for the last minute to do things. We should at least have an idea of the project we want to do."

Indira rolled her eyes and mumbled something about Feng being uptight.

Krystal, ever the peacemaker, chimed in. "You're both right. Feng, midterms will be over next week. Why don't we focus on studying today? Everyone can be thinking of ideas for the project and then we can present them next time we meet. After exams."

Feng and Indira eyed each other, but both nodded.

They studied in silence for a few hours. At the end of the study session, they all reconvened in the big meeting room for final announcements.

"I know everyone is studying, but we still have our homeless outreach this Saturday in midtown," Krystal announced. "I hope you guys will join me."

As of yet, only Bamo and Femi had shown up to help feed on Saturdays, but Krystal faithfully announced it every time they got together.

"After midterms, we're all invited to go to my parents' place at Lake Lanier for celebration and relaxation," Indira announced.

Everyone cheered. Bamo frowned.

"We have a lake house, and we love to take people out on the boat. We'll also have a big barbeque. My dad will hire a van so we can all go together. We can leave early and make a whole day of it. Who's in?"

Everyone raised their hand except Bamo. He looked around the room at everyone looking at him with surprise and slowly lifted his hand.

After everyone had packed up and left, Krystal lingered behind, waiting on him to finish up some notes he had transcribed.

"Bamo, you don't want to go to the lake?"

"Not really. But I'll go to be with everyone else. I think I'll stay in the house and not go out on the boat though."

"Really? I can't wait to get on the boat. I love the water. You don't?"

Bamo shook his head slowly. He and Krystal had talked a lot about her life in Haiti and Panama and his life in Africa. But there were things about his life in Oume he had never shared. She didn't know his mother had died in a flood.

"I don't love water at all." Bamo's voice sounded sadder than he meant it to.

Krystal looked into his eyes. She had a funny way of doing that. It seemed like she could feel when he was upset or worried about something. She put her hand on his arm. "Why not?"

Bamo didn't mean to step back, but he needed to put some space between him and Krystal's eyes. By looking at him that way, she had pulled out some of his deepest and most private thoughts about life back in Oume and the things about his life in America that made him sad or afraid. He couldn't let those eyes dig into his soul because he didn't want to tell her about his mother. His mother lived in a place deep inside his heart that he didn't want to share.

"It's nothing." He shook off her hand on his arm.

Krystal was one of those people that touched all the time. Stephanie was too, but for some reason, Krystal's touch wasn't sweet and comforting like Stephanie's. It always made him feel things he wasn't sure he should feel.

She frowned. Bamo instantly felt bad. The last thing he wanted to do was hurt Krystal. She was the nicest person he had ever met and most of the time he felt like he wanted to protect her innocent heart. The way she wore her heart on the outside of her body, he was sure Krystal got hurt all the time. He didn't want to be the cause of that hurt.

"I'm sorry. It's just that..." Bamo's voice trailed off. No, he couldn't give even Krystal that part of his heart.

"Can I walk you back to your dorm?" Bamo asked.

Krystal's frown disappeared, and that sunshiny smile came back. "Yes, of course."

All the way back to her dorm, Bamo made Krystal laugh by telling her stories of mischievous things he had done as a boy in Oume. A peace offering for not being willing to share about his mother.

"You ate lizards?" Krystal scrunched her face up.

Bamo laughed. "Roasted them until they were crunchy. Just the right amount of salt made them the perfect meal. They don't eat lizards where you grew up?"

They exchanged stories about the crazy things people ate when they were growing up. By the time they got to her dorm, they had laughed and talked and Bamo's chest was feeling that funny, warm feeling again.

Before he knew what was happening, Krystal had wrapped his arms around his neck, pulled him close and kissed his cheek. "Thanks, Bamo. I always enjoy spending time with you." Her smile had more than sunshine in it.

Bamo felt like he couldn't take in enough air, even after she let him go and gave a little wave and disappeared into the dorm.

Chapter 15

Exams were over. It was time for Bamo to meet with his study group to start working on their final class project. He was supposed to be ready to present a possible idea for the project, but he hadn't given it any thought at all. Exams were pretty rigorous. He had hoped they would postpone the meeting so he could have time to at least put an idea together, but Feng had insisted they were already behind schedule.

They had decided to have the meeting at Jason and Stephanie's house so they would have plenty of room to work and could enjoy Stephanie's good food.

His study group all rode together from campus in Indira's Land Cruiser, and they were late, probably because they had to wait for Femi. Seated around his dining table were Krystal, Indira, Feng, Femi, Muthoni from Kenya, and a quiet girl from Cameroon named Eposi.

After they all greeted and exchanged pleasantries, Feng immediately took over. "So, is everyone ready to present their ideas for the project?"

The team had to create a plan for a development project in an underdeveloped country, no matter how small. The assignment was general and vague and left up to the creativity of the students.

Nobody said a word. Bamo guessed everyone had been as overwhelmed with midterms as he was and didn't get a chance to come up with an idea. As the silence extended, a frown crept over Feng's face.

Just as he was about to open his mouth, Krystal spoke, "I'm sure we're all recovering from exams. But the beauty of all these great minds being seated together at the table is that we can come up with an idea on the spot."

Krystal turned to Indira, "What about you? What problem needs solving in the country where you're from?"

Indira frowned and curled up her lip. "I don't know. I've never lived there. My parents moved to America not long after they married. I've visited, but I don't really know the country well enough to plan a project."

Bamo thought it strange that Indira didn't know enough about the problems where she was from to even be able to come up with a project, but he wasn't surprised. That was the kind of person she was.

"Femi, what about you?"

"Yo, I'm from Lekki." Femi was from the well-to-do part of Lagos in Nigeria. "Life is nice where I'm from."

Stephanie came in from the kitchen and put a bowl of tortilla chips and salsa on the table. "Femi, you mean you don't know anything about the issues facing your people in Nigeria? Really?"

Everybody in the group loved Stephanie because she overstuffed them with food every time they came over. She also chimed in with great ideas whenever they were talking about development stuff. She had a degree in development as well, so they considered her an expert in their field.

Femi looked sheepish. "I went to boarding school and then came here. What do I know?"

Muthoni laid out an idea for a program for street kids in Nairobi. "These kids leave terrible home situations and end up living on the street for years. They use drugs, steal, and are often arrested. If we can get them off the street and either back with their families or into a resource home where they can be sent to school, it can change their whole life."

Everyone was nodding their approval at her idea, except Indira. She had a big frown on her face.

"It's so cliché. Everybody does programs for street kids in Kenya."

"Are you serious? What's cliché about helping children get off the street and get an education?" Muthoni snapped.

"We need something more original and different."

"I don't remember you presenting any idea, Miss Indian American Princess."

Krystal jumped in. "Okay, ladies, let's keep it civil. Indira, if you'd like another turn, we'd love to hear any idea that you might have."

Indira said nothing. Just sulked.

"Muthoni, I think it's a great idea. Let's see if anyone else has anything and then we can see which project we can develop the best. Eposi?"

Indira interrupted. "What about you, Krystal? You didn't come with any ideas for the project?"

Bamo wanted to say something to Indira. He wasn't sure what. He didn't want to be mean because that wasn't his character. But he also didn't think she should continue to get away with insulting people and treating them rudely.

Krystal simply smiled. She never seemed to let Indira get to her. She started sharing her idea for a development project for Panama.

Before she could get too far into her idea, Indira interrupted. "Krystal, we know your parents are missionaries, but the project can't be related to any religion. It's not fair for you to expect us to do a Christian project."

"Christian project? How is a farming project for self-sustenance a Christian project?"

"Isn't that what your parents are doing?"

"It's one of the many projects they're involved in, but it has nothing to do with Christianity. Feeding people is feeding people."

Bamo was surprised to hear Krystal's voice rise a little.

Stephanie entered from the kitchen again with 2-liter bottles of

Coke and Sprite. "I'm surprised Bamo hasn't told you of the millions of projects you guys could do in his village, Oume, back on the Ivory Coast. There's such a great need there. A little goes a long way."

All eyes turned toward Bamo.

"Bamo, any ideas?"

Bamo shrugged. He didn't talk much about his life in Oume with the whole group. Even though they were "internationals," most of them came from rich backgrounds. The only person he related to was Chuks, who grew up in a small village in Nigeria.

Stephanie came back with disposable cups and a bowl of ice. "Before she passed away, Bamo's mother had started a school in their village. It's the reason Bamo is so smart and it was changing the lives of many of the children of his village and the surrounding ones."

Everyone turned from Stephanie to Bamo with wide eyes. Bamo shrugged again.

Stephanie continued, "Who knows? If you guys develop a good project, we might be able to get it funded. We could raise money or seek a grant."

Jason and Stephanie had continued to travel to Oume over the years. Bamo had never visited. Bamo missed home, but he'd kept his promise to Chief that he wouldn't come home until he had finished school and become successful in life. Whatever that meant.

"What happened to the school...after Bamo's mom...passed?" Krystal asked.

Bamo couldn't read the look in her eyes. Was she hurt because she didn't know his mother was dead? She'd once she asked about his family. She was curious about how he came to live with Jason and Stephanie. He said he didn't want to talk about it. He said it in such a way that she had never asked again.

"The school is still running, but we...me and Bamo's mom had planned to take it to a whole new level." Stephanie stared into space for a few minutes. "We moved on to other projects after she passed. Without her there, the people were more interested in farming and irrigation projects than building levies. Now that's something that could change life for the villagers."

"Levies?" Krystal and Muthoni asked at the same time.

Stephanie nodded and took a seat at the dining table with them. Bamo wasn't surprised she was interested in helping them with the project. Even though she and Jason still went to Oume once a year, they were less involved. Jason's job had become more time consuming and Stephanie was devoted to her community projects in Atlanta and raising Bamo.

"Every few years, there are heavy rains in Oume and the surrounding villages. The rivers overflow the banks, and there's bad flooding. Many lives are lost because it happens so fast and unexpectedly. That's how Bamo lost his mother."

Stephanie turned to Bamo, looking as if she was just realizing his friends didn't know how his mother had died. Her face was suddenly apologetic.

Bamo looked down at his hands. The room was quiet.

Krystal finally spoke in her soft, gentle voice. "Sorry, Bamo. We didn't know."

There were murmurs of condolence around the rest of the dining table.

There was more silence until Muthoni finally spoke. "You know they say the best projects are those closest to our hearts. People are more passionate about causes that have directly affected them. And this flooding problem has deeply affected you." She put her hand on Bamo's arm. "And because it's affected you, it's affected all of us, right?"

Bamo lifted his eyes and smiled at his friend.

Krystal put her hand on his other arm. "Yeah, because it's affected you, we will all be passionate about it." She looked around the table at the others. "Right, guys?"

Everybody nodded.

Krystal squeezed his arm. "Flooding in Oume. How can we help?"

Bamo took a deep breath and looked around the table at his

friends–no, family–from all over the world. "Yes, how can we help?"

Stephanie sat with them for the next hour, and they discussed various projects that would benefit the people of Oume and the surrounding villages. Not only levies to prevent flooding, but revitalizing Diaka's school, adult literacy programs, and farming and irrigation.

Muthoni was right. The more Bamo described the problems of his village, the more passionate he became about projects that could bring lasting, sustainable change. And the more passionate he became, the more passionate his friends became.

After two hours, they had three plausible projects to improve life in Oume. They made individual assignments for each person to further develop the projects–research, budgeting, feasibility, and planning measurable outcomes.

After everyone left, Krystal lingered behind. Bamo knew she would want to talk about his past. Today, he was willing to talk. Somehow, talking about Oume as a development project made it feel less painful. Maybe the pain was reduced by the feeling that there was actually something he could do about it. Even though every decision he made was toward going back to Oume to help, this was the first time he actually sat and made concrete plans.

Krystal slowly packed her bag. Bamo wasn't surprised she didn't leave with the others. She had forfeited her ride back with Indira, he knew, so she could make sure he was okay.

"So is that why you weren't excited about going to the lake?"

Bamo raised an eyebrow. "Huh?"

"When Indira announced the lake party, we were all excited, but you looked upset. And it was clear you didn't want to go. Now I understand why."

Bamo said, "You don't miss anything, do you?"

Krystal smiled. "Not often."

She stopped packing her bag and looked him in the eyes. "I'm sorry about your mom. I can understand why you didn't want to talk about your family when I asked. I can't imagine..."

Bamo nodded. He didn't have anything to say.

"But I'm glad we're doing the project. Something great can come out of the tragedy. My parents always quote this Scripture about what the enemy meant for evil, God turning it for good. This project could do that."

Bamo shrugged. "It's a class project. An idea. It's not like we have the means to carry it out. We'll do the research, estimate a budget, write up an A plus project and then the class will end and everyone will move on with their lives."

Krystal frowned. "Yes, we'll get an A plus, but that doesn't mean it's only a class project. This is something that can happen, Bamo. It's something that should happen. You never know. We could look for grant funding, submit it and next thing you know, we could be building your mother's school in Oume."

Bamo shrugged.

Krystal gently grabbed his chin and turned his face to look at her. "Bamo, this should happen. You should believe it can. You're always saying you're going to go back and help Oume. Do you really believe it?"

Bamo thought for a second. Did he? It wasn't lost on him that Krystal was saying "we" when referring to looking for grant funding and building his mother's school. What was she saying? Was this more than a class project for her?

Krystal grabbed the plate of chocolate chip cookies Stephanie had put on the table near the end of the meeting. She had fed them so much food that the plate was still half full. Krystal took the plate and planted herself on the couch in the parlor. Bamo guessed she had no intention of calling an Uber any time soon.

He sat on the couch next to her. He waited. He knew it wouldn't be long before she started talking and by the look on her face she wanted to talk about something deep tonight.

"I want to change the world. Don't you, Bamo?"

He nodded.

"Do you actually believe you can though?"

He thought for a second. "I've always planned to. But I never really thought about when or how. I've been too focused on getting an education. And then I'll get a job to start raising money. It may be years before I can do anything in Oume. And I promised my father the chief that I wouldn't come back until I was successful."

"Father, chief?"

Bamo let out a deep breath. Now that Krystal knew the worst part about his painful past, he might as well tell her the rest. He explained that his mother never told him about his father. She simply said that all the men in the village were his father and especially Chief Noumoury. Bamo told Krystal so many stories about what a great man the chief was and how much wisdom he had poured into him over the years.

"He sounds like a great man. I hope to meet him one day."

Bamo looked at her. "You'd come to Ivory Coast?"

"Of course." Krystal threw her arms open wide. "I want to see the whole world."

Bamo laughed. "Do you really believe that's possible?"

Krystal looked deep into his eyes with a determined grin. "My parents raised me to live my life like anything is possible. And that's exactly what I plan to do."

Bamo smiled.

"If you keep hanging around me, I might just have you believing it, too. We could change the world, Bamo, because anything is possible."

There she went with that "we" again. Bamo was sure he was blushing.

Chapter 16

Exams were over, the project was well underway, and it was time to go to the lake. Bamo wasn't excited about the day, but he convinced himself he'd be fine if he just stayed inside the lake house. He wasn't going anywhere near the water.

He was standing at the meeting point waiting for Indira's driver. He had arrived first and Feng and Chuks came soon after. Chuks was as loud and boisterous as Feng was quiet, but for some reason, the two were good friends. Chuks kept everybody laughing all the time, and maybe Feng knew he needed that in his life.

Soon they were joined by Femi, Muthoni, Eposi, and the others.

Krystal was almost the last to arrive. She was dressed in a yellow sundress that looked perfect against her warm brown skin. Her skin color was deep and rich, like his mother's. He often told her that she could easily pass for an Ivorian with her dark skin and thick wooly hair that she wore in different Afro styles. His favorite was when she let it fly free and wild with a colorful scarf tied around it, like today.

The van arrived. They all loaded up and set out for Lake Lanier. Krystal sat next to him and because they were many, she was squeezed a little closer to him than was comfortable. Bamo hoped the trip wasn't too long.

Bamo had never liked a girl before. He was too focused on his studies and making Jason and Stephanie and his whole village proud. But he had gotten to the point that he thought about Krystal all the time. It was becoming distracting.

Right before one of their midterm exams, she had smiled her sunshine smile at him. It took him a good five minutes before he could concentrate on the first question. He couldn't afford to be distracted. He still had the rest of this year and the next before he graduated. He intended to do so with honors.

He kept talking to himself, trying to chase her out of his mind, but nothing seemed to work. And with her pressed up against him in the van for the more than an hour ride to Lake Lanier, things weren't about to get any better.

Indira's parents' lake house was large and beautiful. She led them into a huge room with floor to ceiling windows that framed a pristine picture of a large, peaceful lake. The yard was filled with tall trees with strong branches that looked perfect for climbing. Even though the trees weren't at all similar to the ones you would see in Oume and the lake was still and quiet, unlike the rushing river at the edge of his village, the place still reminded him of home.

The sounds of birds squawking in the trees and the huge wide open sky with no large buildings blocking his view of the sun and the clouds filled his heart. Staring at the water reminded him of all the days he got in trouble when he snuck out to the river with Caleb and Wilfred.

He stood in front of the window, gazing into his past. All sorts of emotions stirred inside of him. He should have followed his first thought and not come. His mind shut out the boisterous conversation and laughter of his friends as he stood gazing at the water, remembering the day he was told his mother was dead.

"Bamo?" Krystal was standing there, touching his arm, staring at him with those eyes of hers. "You okay?"

He shook himself from his past and smiled. "I'm fine. Very fine. This place is beautiful, isn't it?" He tried to smile and nod as if his heart didn't feel like a lead weight inside of his chest. "Let me go and greet Indira. I haven't spoken to her yet and thanked her for inviting us." He abruptly walked away before Krystal could answer.

He found Indira checking the food table. They had set out quite a spread, and they still had to barbeque the meat.

He greeted Indira and extended his thanks, then said, "Do they need any help with the barbeque? I'm very good at it." He had grown up barbequing in the backyard with Jason all summer, every summer.

Indira frowned. "No, Bamo. We have people to do that for us." She curled her upper lip.

"I was only offering to help. You don't have to be so…" Bamo didn't even bother to finish his sentence. Indira never acknowledged when she was rude to people, so what was the point?

Bamo went over and joined Chuks and Femi at the small bar that was set up for them. They were both drinking beers. Bamo chose a Coke. Jason had introduced him to beer and other alcohol, but Bamo didn't like the taste or the fuzzy feeling it gave. Chuks and Femi, on the other hand, would drink until they were both loud and very funny. Bamo hoped their boisterous jokes would help him shake off the lingering feeling of Oume.

After they ate and drank their fill, it was time to get on the boat. Bamo refused at first. He had no desire to go out on any body of water. He was already feeling his past too much. Everyone coaxed and begged him, but he held his ground. He would stay and wait for them at the house.

But as they were getting on to the large beautiful boat, Bamo could hear Chief Noumoury's voice in his head. "A man must never allow his fears to rule his life. When fear is controlling you, run toward it, attack it, and conquer it."

The phrase kept rolling over and over in his head. Just as the boat was about to push off from the pier, Bamo ran to the edge. "Wait for me. I'm coming."

Even though the sight of the water so close made his head feel light and his stomach sick, he forced himself to get on the boat. He would conquer his fears today and not be ruled anymore.

The boat was bigger than Bamo imagined a boat should be. It had an inside area where there were snacks and drinks and people could stand around and talk. There was music playing. It was a party atmosphere. There was a long couch along one side of the boat and then a few chairs on the other side. Outside, there was a large deck all around the boat where people could stand and look out onto the water.

For the first hour or so, Bamo stayed inside, sitting down with his back to the window. Krystal seemed to sense that he needed space and stayed away, glancing over at him every once in a while to see how he was.

Was it enough to be on the boat to say he conquered his fear? In his heart, he knew it wasn't. So Bamo sat facing the window for a while, ignoring the fun conversation among his friends. He then stood up by the window, gazing out as the water glided by.

Finally, he knew what he had to do. He walked outside onto the deck. First, he was glued to the wall. His hands were covered in sweat, and his legs were weak. He chanted over and over in his mind, "Fear will not rule me. Fear will not rule me."

Slowly, he inched further and further away from the wall and finally stood against the rail. Even though he was gripping it so tight that his dark knuckles were white, he was still there. Conquering. He could see Chief Noumoury's eyes beaming with pride.

He stood at the rail, breathing, thankful for the slow speed of the boat. There was another boat coming toward them that was going much faster. There was loud music blasting from it. There were adults on the deck laughing and talking loud. They were having a serious party. Bamo thought it dangerous for them to be going so fast.

As the boat got closer, Bamo felt nervous and went back to standing on the wall. He knew the boats couldn't crash, but somehow the wall made him feel safe. The boat sped by and seemed as if it was flying. Bamo knew the people on that boat were ten times richer than Indira's parents. The boat was huge and looked expensive. There were adults in scant clothing scattered on the deck with drinks in their hands. At the back of the boat, there was a group of young boys playing near the railing.

Bamo peeled himself off the wall. If children could play on the deck of a boat near the rail, then what was he afraid of? He took some more deep breaths and went back to the rail. This time he leaned on it instead of gripping it. "I will not fear. I will not fear."

He stayed there on that rail until his heart wasn't beating fast anymore. The big boat with the rich people on it was speeding towards them again. Bamo refused to leave the rail. This time he waved a hand at one little boy who had been left alone at the back of the boat. The boy, who couldn't have been more than five years old, smiled and waved back, leaning against the rail. Before he could blink, Bamo saw the little boy fall over into the water.

His heart gripped. The music on the other boat was so loud they couldn't hear Bamo's screams. Bamo banged on the window of his own boat to get the attention of any of his friends that could come help. As he watched the little boy flailing in the water, Bamo lost all fear or thoughts of himself. He did the only thing he knew to do. He plunged into the water to save the little boy.

The icy water startled him. He shook off his initial reaction to the cold, swam toward the little boy, and grabbed his arm. The little boy kept flailing and then put his arms around Bamo's head, covering his eyes and smothering his nose. He kept kicking his legs. Bamo couldn't understand how a boy so small could be so strong. It felt like he would take them both under.

Bamo remembered when the older boys in the village were teaching the younger ones to swim in the river. He remembered fighting so hard one day that one of the older boys clipped him in the chest and let him go. The boy came behind him and grabbed him, pinning his arms to his side. The boy had yelled into his ear, "Be still or you'll drown us both."

Bamo did the same thing with the little boy. He had to yell a couple of times to get him to stop squirming and it took all his strength to hold the boy's arms. Bamo looked back toward Indira's boat. Thankfully, his friends were standing at the rail, yelling his name. Femi threw a round lifesaver out to him. Chuks jumped off the boat and swam over to them.

"Give me the boy. I'll swim back with him."

Bamo shook his head. "He's too strong. He fights too hard. Grab the lifesaver and help pull us in."

The other friends pulled them up onto the boat. Feng had a large blanket coat looking thing he draped over Bamo and the little boy. Bamo pointed to the boat, speeding away on the river, unaware that it had lost its precious cargo. "Hail, that boat. He fell off of it."

Bamo and the boy were both shaking, teeth chattering. It felt like the cold had gotten into his bones. His head felt heavy and tight. He could barely get air into his chest. He could only think of his mother.

Is that what she felt the moments before she died? The icy grip of death, bringing a fear that saturated the depths of the soul? He cried uncontrollably. His poor mother. What a terrible way to die.

How had he been able to save this little boy, but no one was there to save her?

"Bamo, it's okay. You're fine. The boy is fine. Stop crying." Krystal knelt down beside him, rubbing his arm through the blanket coat.

He could hear her voice but couldn't hear her words. All he heard were the loud cries of the boy. And his own loud cries.

"Bamo!"

Everybody gathered around him, but he refused to be comforted. Nothing could stop the flow of tears and the heavy sobs coming from his belly. He cried so hard he couldn't breathe. Bamo cried until everything went black.

Chapter 17

The next morning, Bamo awoke to find himself snugly tucked into his bed at Jason and Stephanie's house. He sat up in bed and frowned, not remembering how he got there. He shook his head and tried to capture the events of the day before. A sick feeling of dread came over him as he remembered the incident on the boat. He remembered being told that he and the little boy he had saved were fine, but everything after that was blurry.

The night had been full of dark dreams. He had hardly dreamed about his mother since he left Oume. On Christmas or when some big event happened in his life, he would dream about her, but those were happy dreams, from happy memories.

He had felt sad every time he got an award in school, and at his graduation ceremonies from middle and high school. He was sad she wasn't there to see him and for her chest to expand with pride at the things her son was accomplishing. But then at night, when he fell asleep, she visited him in his dreams, always smiling, always laughing, and always telling him how proud she was of everything he was becoming. Those were his favorite dreams, and he hated waking up from them.

The dreams of the night before had not been kind. He had felt the icy grip of death holding him under the water. He had seen his mother under the water. She was stuck, her face twisted and contorted from struggling for air, struggling for life. And she kept calling his name—over and over and over. He could still hear her voice. He knew from the way she called his name that what she hated the most about dying was leaving him behind, just as her mother had left her behind and their mother before that.

His heart ached inside his chest. He wanted to get up and go for a run, to see if he could get away from the heavy, sad feeling that didn't want to lift. But as he moved his limbs to get out of the bed, he still felt the soreness from struggling with the little boy and being submerged in the cold water the day before. He lay back in bed and stared at the ceiling.

He saw Chief Noumoury's face in his mind. So much for conquering his fear. He had only made it worst. He should have never gone out on that boat.

But if he hadn't gone out on the boat, would anyone have been out there to save the little boy's life?

There was a knock on the door. Jason popped his head in. "Bamo, are you awake?"

"Yes, sir."

Jason came over and sat on the edge of Bamo's bed, concern lines etched into his face. "Are you okay, Buddy? I know yesterday was a really difficult day."

Bamo shrugged. Just as Jason was about to ask another question, the doorbell rang.

"Let me get that. Stephanie went out to the store."

Jason disappeared. Moments later, Bamo heard Krystal's voice. He rolled over toward the wall. He didn't want her seeing him so torn and upset. It made him feel weak and vulnerable in front of her, and he didn't like that feeling. Jason always told him that the strength of a real man is being able to show their weakness, but Bamo wasn't sure he agreed with that.

Jason stuck his head in the door again. "Buddy, there's someone here to see you. You might want to brush your teeth and put on a nice shirt." There was a hint of teasing in Jason's voice.

The first time Bamo had hosted one of his study group's monthly dinners at Jason and Stephanie's house, Krystal had been among those who attended. The next day, Stephanie had asked about her and mentioned that she thought Krystal was "sweet on him"—whatever that meant.

Ever since then, Bamo tried to never mention her name because he couldn't keep his face from flushing when he talked about Krystal in front of them. And Jason and Stephanie got too excited at the thought that Bamo might have a girlfriend. He always reassured them that he didn't want anything disrupting his studies, but they always talked about relationships being healthy for a young man of his age.

Bamo forced his long, lanky body out of the bed and went into the bathroom to brush his teeth. He stared at himself hard in the mirror. "Get yourself together, Bamo." He pushed his twisted emotions deep down inside his belly as he dressed in a t-shirt and jeans. He splashed on a little cologne before going down to the parlor to meet Krystal.

As soon as he appeared in the doorway, she jumped up from the couch and next thing he knew, her arms were circling his neck.

"Bamo, are you okay? I was so worried about you yesterday."

He and Krystal had gone from handshakes to sharing brief hugs, but she was clinging to him now. He stood awkwardly with his arms at his sides for a few seconds, but didn't want to hurt her feelings, so he put his arms around her. She clung to him tighter.

Bamo looked over at Jason, hoping for some sort of rescue from the long hug, but Jason smirked and slipped out of the room. Krystal buried her face in Bamo's neck. Her soft, spongy hair smelled like the passion fruit and mangoes from his village. A manly stirring Bamo fought hard to keep at bay whenever he was around Krystal rose up within him. He gently pushed her away.

"Krystal, I'm fine." He gave her a reassuring smile as he took in her beauty.

Bamo, get yourself together. A different kind of weakness made him talk to himself this time.

"Are you sure? You were so upset yesterday. You saved that little boy's life. It was wonderful, but I know it brought back painful memories. I'm so sorry."

Krystal's eyes tried to stare into his soul—into his past—and he quickly looked down at the floor. He led her to the couch to sit down.

"I was afraid for the little boy's life. It was scary that a child could have died."

"Is that all?" Krystal grabbed Bamo's chin and forced him to look at her.

He was saved by the sound of the door leading from the garage to the kitchen opening and Stephanie's voice pouring in, "A little help with these groceries?"

Bamo jumped up from the couch to help. After all the bags were in, Krystal came into the kitchen to greet Stephanie. They shared a hug and a smile.

"So good to see you again, Krystal. So very good. Thanks for coming to see Bamo. He's so lucky to have such a good friend like you. I'm sure your being here will help him recover from yesterday. Such an awful thing for him to have to experience."

Bamo cleared his throat and gave Stephanie a glare behind Krystal's back. Stephanie smirked and started unloading groceries into the refrigerator.

Jason came into the kitchen. "Um, Bamo, the father of the young boy from yesterday is on his way over. He wants to thank you."

Bamo frowned. "He doesn't have to do that. But I guess it's nice of him to come."

Jason scratched his head. "Apparently it's more than him being nice. I couldn't quite figure out what he was saying, but he wanted to know if there was any special way he could thank you. He also said something about not talking to the media. I'm not sure what's going on."

"The media?" Bamo asked. "From the looks of the boat, the man is rich. I wonder if he's famous as well."

Jason, Krystal and Bamo went to sit in the parlor and chatted while waiting on the visitor. When the doorbell rang, Jason answered it.

A tall, muscular black man with long dreadlocks in a Mohawk style entered the parlor first. His neck and the part of his arms not covered with his shirt were decorated in tattoos. He was followed by a serious looking tall, white woman with bright red hair. She had on a well-fitted, expensive looking suit and a tight-lipped frown. The man's head was hung down. It was funny to look at them, almost like the tall, muscular man was a child in trouble with an angry mother.

Krystal gasped. "OMG! Deonte Barrett?"

The man lifted his head, smiled, and nodded a return greeting.

Krystal squealed. "OMG! Are you serious?" She turned to Bamo. "He plays for the Atlanta Hawks!"

Bamo's eyes widened. No wonder the man was so tall and muscular. He knew the man must have been rich from the party on the boat, but he never guessed he'd be an NBA player. They all shook hands with the man.

"Thanks so much for saving my son's life yesterday. I can't tell you how much..." Deonte Barrett stood there silent for a second, shaking his head, like he was full of the same level of emotion Bamo had been feeling since the day before.

Bamo bowed his head. "You're welcome, sir. I'm glad I could help. The boy is fine?"

Deonte nodded. "Very fine. I left DJ playing a video game at home today. My doctor checked him out at the house last night. He's perfectly fine. I have you to thank for that. Thank you." His voice choked a little again. He kept shaking Bamo's hand vigorously.

Bamo nodded. He wasn't sure what to do with himself. He introduced Krystal, Jason, and Stephanie.

Stephanie shook his hand and asked, "So nice to meet you. Please make yourself comfortable."

She gestured for Deonte to have a seat. Which left everyone staring at the red-headed woman who hadn't spoken since they'd entered.

It was strange how fast her face went from the tight frown to a smile—not a warm smile from a good heart, but a smile that made you wonder what was coming next. "I'm Sarah Thornton, Mr. Barrett's publicist. So nice to meet all of you and thanks for agreeing to see Mr. Barrett on such short notice."

Stephanie nodded and gestured for her to sit as well.

Sarah sat on the edge of the armchair. "We won't take up a lot of your time." She spoke to Bamo. "Mr. Barrett wanted to express his thanks for your heroic act yesterday. What thanks can one actually give for someone saving their child's life?" She glared at Deonte Barrett for a brief second and his head dropped again.

She turned back to Bamo. "He would like to do more than just express his thanks in words. I understand you're in your junior year of college?"

Bamo nodded.

"Mr. Barrett would like to pay off the rest of your college tuition and fees. A check can be sent to the university this week."

Bamo's mouth dropped open. He shook himself, remembering, "But I'm on full scholarship."

Sarah frowned and tapped her chin, thinking. "Well, then he can just write the check directly to you. Maybe you'd like to buy yourself a car or some designer clothes or deck out your room with a flat screen and the latest Xbox or something." She pulled out her phone. "Please tell me the correct spelling of your name?"

"I don't want or need any of those things." Bamo was mute for a few seconds, then he spoke to Deonte. "You don't have to pay me for saving your son's life. Any decent human being would have done the same."

Deonte's head was still down.

"Of course." Sarah spoke even though Bamo had addressed Deonte. "Let's not think of it as paying you to save DJ's life. It's more of an expression of gratitude. And..."

Everyone turned toward Sarah Thornton.

"And a way of asking for your discretion in this matter. There's no way you could possibly imagine how difficult it is to live a...public life. Anything that happens, people always ask questions and make judgments. Even though this was a private and personal crisis for Mr. Barrett, people will want to know what happened."

"You mean they'll want to know why DJ was at the back of the boat all alone?" Bamo finally asked the question that had been bothering him the whole morning.

Sarah's plastic smile receded back into the tight frown again as she glared at Deonte. "Yes. Exactly. And that would make this personal, private crisis even more painful for Mr. Barrett."

Deonte covered his face with one of his large hands. Bamo couldn't imagine the shame he was feeling.

Sarah cleared her throat. "As you may be aware, Mr. Barrett has had some...difficult situations lately. He's been in and out of quite a bit of...trouble lately and..." she let out a deep breath. "The press has not been kind to him. So if we could avoid this situation adding to his negative press...that would be...greatly appreciated."

Everyone was quiet for a few moments.

Sarah finally spoke, her tone more humble, almost pleading. "So, as I said. The check isn't for saving DJ's life. It's more to save Deonte's."

Bamo nodded, but it felt strange to take the man's money. And what exactly was Sarah Thornton asking him to do? He didn't have to wonder long.

"We hope that this situation hasn't become known. But if it has, the media will contact you. If they do, they'll ask a lot of questions about what happened yesterday. You could refuse to give any statement at all. If you choose to talk, it would be great if you didn't mention exactly how things happened yesterday."

Bamo frowned. "Are you asking me to lie?"

Sarah's face became strained. "Lie? No. I wouldn't ask you to lie. What I'm asking you is..." She tapped her chin. "I'm asking you not to help the media make a negative case against Mr. Barrett. They'll paint him as an irresponsible parent. If they add the 'trouble' he's gotten into lately, things could really look bad for him as a father. You wouldn't want that, would you?"

Bamo looked at Deonte. He wouldn't want to make him look bad as a father. The truth was the truth. The boy had been alone at the back of a speeding boat. They hadn't even noticed that he had fallen into the water and been rescued. They'd had to radio the boat, and it took a while for them to come back and get DJ. So it wouldn't be Bamo's fault if Deonte looked like a bad father.

He didn't want to talk to the media though. He didn't understand the way the American press liked to destroy people. He wanted no part of that ugly process.

Sarah stared at him hard, and he wondered what she was thinking. She finally spoke, "Well, I'm happy you're on full scholarship." She looked around the house. "Your foster parents seem to be doing really well, but aren't you from Africa? Don't you have some poor relatives back home that need help? You might not need anything but I'm sure they do."

Stephanie stood and put a hand on her hip. "Now wait just a minute." The anger on her face made Bamo know Sarah was about to get an earful. "You have a lot of nerve coming in here, asking Bamo to lie for Mr. Barrett for money to send back to Africa. We don't need your money. Who do you think—"

Jason pulled at Stephanie's arm to calm her down.

Krystal, who had been quiet for some time, spoke up. "Ms. Thornton, I think I have an idea for how Mr. Barrett can 'express his gratitude' and also improve his press."

Sarah Thornton turned to her with an eager look on her face. "I'm listening."

Chapter 18

B amo sat on the couch almost in complete shock. Once Sarah Thornton responded with a bit of interest, Krystal started talking and kept talking. Bamo had seen the sunshiny, sweet side of his friend, but today, he saw how powerful she could be. She and Sarah had gone back and forth, around and around, discussing terms until they finally came to an agreement.

"See, Bamo, I told you to believe! I told you anything is possible!" Krystal was dancing around the parlor on her toes.

Bamo nodded, but still hadn't grasped what had just happened.

By the time they ushered Sarah and Deonte Barrett to the door, their Oume development project was no longer an A plus assignment. It was a reality.

"I can't believe it. One hundred thousand dollars?" Bamo shook his head.

"That's pocket change to him. I promise you, he won't even miss it."

"This is incredible, Buddy," Jason chimed in. "Absolutely incredible. Krystal, I can't believe you did that."

Stephanie was sitting next to Bamo almost in shock as much as he was. A tear slid down her cheek. "I can't believe it." She put a hand on Bamo's back. "You know what this means, don't you? We can finally build the school your mother dreamed of."

Bamo frowned. "But will it be enough?"

Krystal stopped dancing and put her hands on her hips. "Are you serious? You're still doubting? If the check he gives us isn't enough, we'll raise the rest. Didn't you hear the rest of the conversation, or did your ears stop hearing after they agreed to the hundred thousand?"

"I heard you talking about a social media campaign. Is that how you plan to raise the money?"

"Yesss!" Krystal said the word long and drawn out, almost mocking him. "NBA star Deonte Barrett is going to lend his fame to your campaign for Oume. Instead of a smear campaign exposing him as a horrible father that leaves his child unattended on a fast-moving party boat, we're going to spin it for Oume's good."

She put her hands in a television screen frame and stared through it. "Young African man risks his life to rescue NBA star, Deonte Barrett's, son from drowning at Lake Lanier. Deonte Barrett is grateful and wants to hear the story of this young African man who has survived a life of poverty and hardship and become a successful student on full scholarship at Emory University.

"Mr. Barrett is so moved by the resilience and tenacity of this young African man that he wants to help. He's so moved that this young African man pushed past his fears of water and drowning after the loss of his mother in the floods in his village in the Ivory Coast and he wants to make sure that never happens to another child in that village. Deonte Barrett is not only helping to build levies to prevent floods, he's also rebuilding the school started by the young African man's mother before she died. In fact, she gave her life trying to build the school—the same school that made this young African man into the amazing student that he is now. Now this young African man can continue his mother's dream and help other young African men become amazing students who can change the world."

Bamo frowned. "Do you have to say 'young African man' so many times?"

Krystal nodded. "Africa is 'in' now and we're going to capitalize on that."

Bamo winced. "It's not like Africa is a country."

Krystal nodded again. "I've been a missionary kid all my life,

Bamo. Fundraising is not for the faint of heart. We do what we have to in order to support the cause. As long as it's honest and ethical. It takes money to change the world and sometimes people have to be convinced that they want to be a part of bringing about that change."

Stephanie laughed. She stood and hugged Krystal. "You remind me so much of me when I was your age. To be young and idealistic again."

"Ms. Stephanie, this is about to be awesome beyond our wildest dreams. Just you watch."

"Oh, I believe you dear. I believe you with all my heart." Stephanie grabbed her by the hand. "Let's go make some tea and some plans." She ushered her into the kitchen.

Jason popped up from the armchair and came over to the couch to sit next to Bamo. "You okay, Buddy?"

Bamo nodded slowly.

"Are you okay with sharing your mother's story? I know you never talk about it. Stephanie said you hadn't even mentioned it to your close friends. Are you sure you're going to be okay with sharing it with the world of social media?"

Bamo stroked his chin slowly, thinking. "I think so. I hope so. If it will help raise money for Oume, then I should, right?"

"Only if you're comfortable with it."

Bamo nodded, still stroking his chin and thinking. "Do you think it's wrong? What Krystal just said? What she just did with Ms. Thorton and Mr. Barrett?"

Jason chuckled. "Wrong?" He clapped Bamo on the back. "I think Krystal is a very smart girl. A passionate woman and a resourceful one. I think what she just did was brilliant. I can't believe how she pulled it off with a sweet smile on her face."

Jason looked hard at Bamo. "If you're smart, you'll keep her around. She could take you places."

Bamo furrowed his eyebrows. "What do you mean? Keep her around?"

Jason laughed loud. "Come on, Buddy. You know what I mean.

I've seen the way you look at Krystal and the way she looks at you. I know you're focused on your studies and all, but don't be so focused that you miss something amazing." He leaned back to look into the kitchen to make sure the women were occupied.

He continued. "Stephanie is right. Krystal is a lot like her. Passionate, pure-hearted, focused, and beautiful. You don't find that combination often. In fact, how many women like Krystal have you met?"

Bamo thought for a second. "None. None at all."

"Well, there you go. That tells you everything you need to know."

"It does?"

Jason rolled his eyes like Bamo was dull and slow. "Yes, it does. She's one of a kind. You may never meet another like her, so you better hold on to her."

"Hold on to her how?"

Jason flopped back on the couch and stared at the ceiling. "Seriously? Have I taught you so much, but yet taught you so little?"

Bamo smirked.

"Hmmm...maybe Stephanie and I encouraged you too much on education without teaching you about other important things." He let out a long sigh. "I think it's time for a man-to-man talk."

Bamo covered his face with his hands. "Oh no, not again."

Jason laughed. Not long after Bamo had moved to America, at around age fifteen, Jason insisted they talk about sex and manhood. Bamo had been mortified. Nobody ever talked of such things where he was from. People just grew up and things happened. There was never any awkward talk about it. But Jason had made sure they had plenty "man-to-man talks" over the years. When it came to things like planning for the future, how to treat women with respect, and how to manage finances, Bamo thoroughly enjoyed their talks. But when it was the more awkward topics, Bamo wanted to run. He was sure this was going to be one of those awkward talks.

"You know Stephanie was my first and only girlfriend. I've told you that, haven't I?"

Bamo nodded.

"It's a great thing. Never got my heart broken, never had to break up a relationship. I chose well the first time and we've been happy ever since. Maybe it's good that you've never been in a relationship."

Bamo nodded. He hoped if he didn't say a word, this would be over sooner rather than later.

"Krystal is that kind of girl. The kind that when you see her, you grab her up and never take the chance of anyone else getting her. It's a great thing that you wanted to graduate college without any distractions, but Krystal isn't a distraction. She's the kind of woman that builds you and helps you. I'm telling you, that's a good woman that you don't want to let go of."

Bamo blushed and put his head down.

"You're awful quiet, Buddy. This is supposed to be a man-to-man talk. Not just a one-man-talking talk."

Bamo shrugged. "I don't know what to say."

"You like her, right?"

Bamo nodded.

"And you know she likes you?"

Bamo shrugged. But he did know. He'd have to be stupid not to know.

"Well, she does. She really, really does. What's keeping you from going for it?"

"I don't know how to go for it. I don't know what to say or what to do."

Jason chuckled. He sat and thought for a second. "Just be honest. Tell her how you feel. And whatever you do, don't let her get away."

Bamo let out a deep sigh. Jason kept saying that, and he had to admit the thought had crossed his mind. When he was conquering his fears on the boat, he had seen Chuks approach Krystal several times trying to talk to her. Bamo could see her being friendly, but then she kept moving away to another part of the boat. At one of their previous study groups, Chuks had come in late and squeezed his chair in next to Krystal's, wedging his way in between her and Bamo.

Bamo had seethed for half the meeting. Krystal was a beautiful girl. What if he couldn't find a way to tell her how he felt about her and somebody else did? He didn't like that thought.

"What do I say?"

Jason clapped him on the back. "Just be honest. It's not that hard, Bamo. Tell her you like her. Tell her you want to be with her."

Bamo's eyes bugged out. How could he say that? The thought made him tremble.

Jason laughed. "Seriously? You can't be scared. Think of all the things you've overcome and conquered in this life. This is a piece of cake compared to that."

Not to him. Telling Krystal how he felt about her was the scariest thing he had ever faced.

Stephanie and Krystal reemerged from the kitchen.

"I better head back to campus. I've got some laundry and stuff to do before school tomorrow. Bamo, I'm so excited about everything that happened today. I can't wait to tell the rest of our project group. They're not going to believe this!"

Bamo nodded, now completely unable to talk to Krystal at all.

Jason spoke up. "Bamo, don't you need to be heading back to campus too? You guys could share an Uber." Jason looked at him intently.

Bamo gulped. The thought of riding in a car back to campus with Krystal was suddenly terrifying. What would they say? Would she know the talk he and Jason just had?

"Yeah, let me pack you guys some food to go. Go ahead and request the Uber. You know it'll be a little while before they get here."

Krystal tapped away at her phone while Bamo tried to think of an excuse to go back to campus later. Alone.

Jason pulled him out of his thoughts. "Do you need to grab anything from your room before you go? I think you only came here from the boat with the clothes you were wearing. They're in the laundry. You can get them next time you come."

Bamo nodded.

Krystal looked up from her phone. "Five minutes away. They must have been close. Cool."

Stephanie came in from the kitchen with a bag of food. "Here you go."

Bamo was quiet the whole Uber ride back to campus. Luckily, Krystal was still excited from the events of the morning so she spent the whole time chattering a mile a minute about their project and everything they could do in Oume.

When they got to campus, they stopped in front of Krystal's dorm.

"Do you want to hang out for a little while? I can throw a load of laundry in the wash and then we can talk some more."

Bamo shook his head. "I better get back to my room. I have to..." Any possible excuse to not spend any more time with Krystal escaped him.

"You have to what?" Krystal took one step closer to Bamo and looked him in the eyes.

He coughed.

"You have to what? Come on, Bamo. You don't have anywhere to go or anything to do. Come hang out with me." She grabbed his hand and started leading him toward her dorm building.

He stopped her and blurted out, "Krystal...I like you very much. Very, very much. Okay? I want you to be my girlfriend." Bamo's heart was pounding in his chest.

Krystal's face lit up with a huge smile. She laughed and threw her arms around Bamo's neck. She gave him a big kiss on the cheek. "Finally. I thought you'd never ask."

Bamo laughed. "What?"

Krystal kissed his cheek again. "I thought I was going to have to ask you."

Bamo laughed even louder. "You were going to ask me?"

Krystal nodded. "Yeah, you were taking too long."

Krystal laid her head on his chest and Bamo kicked himself for not asking her sooner. "Sorry, I took too long. But thanks for saying yes."

"Oh, Bamo. It's okay." Krystal laughed and then looked him in the eyes. She smiled up at him. "We're going to change the world."

Chapter 19

Bamo couldn't believe it had been five years since he and Krystal had launched Build Oume, their nonprofit for relief and development of Oume and the surrounding villages. They had graduated from Emory undergrad and both had completed Master's degrees.

Bamo had interned with Habitat for Humanity during the summer of his junior year at Emory and throughout his senior year. He had been hired after graduation and had worked there for two years, gleaning everything he could on how to run a nonprofit and do development in impoverished countries.

Krystal had taken a job at Operation Mobilization, a missions organization serving missionaries in one hundred and eighteen different nations. She did everything from fundraising to social media to management of missionaries out in the field.

Both of them knew that God had provided the perfect jobs to train them for their future work in Oume. They didn't make the highest salaries, but the skills they were developing were completely priceless for their dream of "changing the world." Bamo had moved back home with Jason and Stephanie and Krystal lived in a small apartment in the next suburb over so they could save every extra cent they made.

The nonprofit was thriving. Deonte Barrett helped with the social media campaign for about six months as promised, but after that, Bamo became the face of the organization. Krystal used her writing skills to help him create compelling stories of his life in Oume and the needs of the people there.

Bamo had discovered a side of himself he didn't know existed. At first, he was nervous talking in front of the camera, but with Krystal's words and sunny encouragement, he became friends with the camera. Now he could shoot videos without a thought. He had a WorldTube channel with almost a million subscribers.

Sometimes he shot videos about life back in the Ivory Coast. Other times he had friends from other African countries sharing about their childhood experiences. Other times, he talked about life in America as an African and everything that came with it. Krystal was always coming up with good ideas for the shows. Just when Bamo thought they had talked about everything they could talk about, she came up with something new.

Jason and Stephanie had started traveling to Oume regularly again. On one of their visits, they took a drone and a high definition camera. They captured really good footage of Oume. They had even gotten shots of the river overflowing its banks in rainy season a couple years back. Those videos with stories of people that had lost their family members in Oume had brought in lots of donations.

They had sent over many containers of books and supplies and had started the building project for Diaka's school. They had implemented farming programs that increased the productivity of Oume and the other villages by more than double. They had a safe water project that was providing a steady supply of clean drinking water to Oume and the surrounding villages.

They were still dreaming of how to make a medical clinic and the levy project a reality. They had written out all the plans for the medical clinic. They had looked at the funds in their nonprofit account, and there just wasn't enough. They needed about half a million dollars to make it happen.

That kind of figure used to scare Bamo but being around Krystal and her strong faith and never-ending optimism changed him. Like her, he had started to believe that anything was possible. He had come to realize that God was with them in everything they did for Oume. It was just a matter of how He would bring the provision. Bamo never doubted He would.

One day, Bamo received a phone call from a strange international number. When he answered, he instantly recognized the voice.

"Bamo!"

He recognized his friend's voice. "Caleb!"

Bamo had been watching his friend's career over the last few years. Jason had continued to encourage him, and Caleb had indeed become a younger version of Drogba. He was playing football in the French League for Paris Saint-Germain F.C. Bamo watched his matches as often as he could. Sometimes he couldn't believe his friend was living his dream.

"I can't believe it's you."

Bamo laughed. "I can't believe it's you."

They chatted for a few minutes to catch up in loud, fast French. Bamo kept saying over and over how proud he was of Caleb and couldn't believe the amazing things that were happening in his life.

"I can't believe what you're doing for Oume. You always said you would and now you're doing it."

"You know about our work in Oume?"

"Are you kidding me? I'm one of your subscribers. I've watched every single video you've done."

Bamo's mouth fell open.

"I'm just mad I had to stumble across it accidentally. I was trying to show my girl where I was from and typed in Oume in the WorldTube search engine. Guess what I found? Those drone videos were amazing. I almost cried from homesickness."

"Wow. I can't believe it."

"I can't believe you didn't tell me what you were doing. You know I'd do anything to help Oume. In fact, that's why I'm calling. I rallied some of my teammates and people from other teams.

We've put a little something together for home. I need to know how to get it to your organization."

Bamo's mouth fell open again. "Seriously, bro?"

"Of course!"

They chatted for a little longer and finished the conversation with Bamo, promising to email the nonprofit's info for the donation.

"Now that you've got my number, let's stay in touch. I've missed you, bro," Caleb said.

"Me too. Oume brothers for life."

The next day, Bamo woke up to three missed calls from Krystal. He called her back. The minute she picked up the phone, she screamed.

"Bamo, oh my God!"

He bolted up in bed. "Krystal, what is it?"

"There was a huge donation sent to our account. Somebody gave us a million dollars!" She screamed over and over and over. He could hear her crying.

Bamo couldn't believe it. Caleb and his football friends had given them a million dollars?

They could build their medical clinic. He lay back in the bed and yelled at the top of his lungs, "Thank you, God!"

And if God had provided for the medical clinic, He would do so for the levies as well.

Over the next few weeks, they met and strategized about how best to use the money and how to build the medical clinic and liaise with the government to get the levies done. Both would require a lot of interaction with the government and with the chiefs of the area. They had a lot of conversations by phone and Skype. They were having difficulty finding contractors they could actually trust to do the work.

Bamo was all too familiar with the fact that corruption was the norm in many African countries. Many times, when given funding for a project, contractors would use less than optimal supplies in order to keep money in their pockets. New roads were full of potholes within a year of being laid. Buildings sometimes collapsed or had major plumbing or electrical problems because of cheap materials.

Bamo didn't want to send over large amounts of money for the hospital project, only to have them build a substandard building that would require costly maintenance and even rebuilding. He didn't want to start the levy project only for a contractor to cut corners to keep back money, leaving the villages at no less risk for flooding. He, Jason, Stephanie, and Krystal had gone over and over how they could best get both projects done. Jason talked about taking some time off work so he and Stephanie could spend more time in Oume, meeting with contractors and making plans.

One night while Bamo was lying awake in bed, the answer came to him. It was time to go home.

He had finished all the education he planned to get. He loved school, but he had no intention of teaching in a university, so there was no need to pursue a PhD. He was successful–not in the way Chief might have meant–with a big job paying lots of money or a big house and many cars. That wasn't his idea of success. Bamo had achieved his idea of success. He was now equipped with the wisdom and skills needed to help the people of rural Ivory Coast. And he had a thriving nonprofit that could fund the projects his wisdom and skills created. What more was there to do in America?

Yes. It was time to go home. His heart started beating as he finalized the decision deep down in his soul. He was going home to Ivory Coast. He was going home to Oume.

First, he had to tell Jason and Stephanie. That wouldn't be hard. They had tried to persuade him to go with them on their last trip to Oume. He didn't know why then, but he didn't feel like it was the right time. Now he knew. When he went back to Oume, it would be to stay.

He would tell them over Saturday morning breakfast.

Stephanie had fixed pancakes, eggs and sausage. Bamo was all too ready to eat. After he, Jason and Stephanie had finished their fill of breakfast, they all sat back in their chairs making small talk for a little while.

Finally, Bamo said, "So there's something I need to tell you guys."

Stephanie and Jason looked at each other, smiled, and looked back at him.

"Yes, Bamo." Stephanie's eyes lit up as she propped her chin on her hands, giving him her full attention.

"I've been thinking a lot about my life and everything that's happened since I came here. First of all, I want to say thank you to the two of you. My life has turned out far more amazing than anything I could have imagined when I first met you in Oume. You've given me a brilliant opportunity. I hope I've made you proud."

Smiling proudly, they both nodded.

"I think you know that even before I got here, it was always my plan to go back to the Ivory Coast. I wanted to come here, get an education and gain skills and knowledge that could help my people. I thought I would work for years and years to be able to raise enough money to do projects in Oume, but God saw fit to accelerate the process. As you both know—"

"You're ready to go back to Oume?" Stephanie exclaimed.

"Let the man finish his speech, Stephanie." Jason interjected.

Stephanie rolled her eyes. "We could be here all day."

Stephanie and Jason laughed.

Bamo laughed with them. "Yes. Yes, I believe it's time to move back to Oume."

Stephanie reached across the table and took Bamo's hands in hers. "Bamo, you've made us so proud. And I'm so excited about the decision you've made. I believe it's time. You know that you have our full support, forever and always."

Jason asked, "So what does that lady of yours think about this?"

Bamo frowned. "I haven't told her yet. I'm on my way over to her place when I leave here. I'm not even sure what to say."

"Just be honest and tell her—"

"I know. Just tell her how I feel." Bamo fingered the old, worn wallet he'd shoved into his pocket before coming downstairs. He didn't know how Krystal would feel about his news. He hoped they'd be okay.

∽∞∾

Things had gone well with Jason and Stephanie, but Bamo wasn't sure how Krystal would react to his decision about moving back to Oume. Ever since that first project meeting where they'd made their first plans for how to help Oume, Krystal had always used the word, "we." As their relationship continued and their nonprofit grew faster and bigger than they had ever imagined, she still always said, "we."

He wondered if the "we" was for their work in the United States. Krystal always talked about seeing Oume and meeting his family there, but was that just for a visit? In order for him to implement the next phase of their programs, Bamo knew he needed to be on the ground in Ivory Coast for extended periods of time. Until everything was launched, he had no choice.

Would they have to have a long-distance relationship? Would he have to travel back and forth to be with Krystal? Would she be willing to visit his home country more than once?

All these questions plagued him on the twenty-minute drive to her apartment. He let out a deep breath as he got out of the car and walked to her door. All he could do was be honest, tell her how he felt, and hope for the best.

When she came to the door, bright and beautiful in a pink top and a pair of jeans, she greeted him with her signature smile. Bamo took her into his arms for a long hug. Could he handle living away from Krystal for months at a time? When she planted a soft kiss on his lips, he knew the answer. He couldn't. But would she be willing to move with him?

"Is everything okay? Your voice sounded funny when you said

you wanted to come over." Krystal's ability to read his every thought and mood had only grown over their past five years together. Sometimes it was unnerving because she figured out what was going on inside of him before he did. But it was comforting to be so well known and so well understood.

"Everything's okay. There's just something I need to talk to you about."

"Okay, come on in." She led him into her parlor, and they sat down on her couch. He loved the way she had decorated her small place. The yellow walls reflected her sunshiny personality. The couch was a calming pink with green and orange throw pillows. He wondered if her love for many colors was from the places she had grown up in, or was it that she was just a colorful person inside?

She studied his face. "What is it?"

He took her hand in his. "Krystal, you know I love you very much, yes?"

She nodded. "Yes. I do. And I love you very much, too."

"Okay, well..." Bamo let out a deep breath. He looked around the room, almost as if he expected the words he needed to be written on those yellow walls somewhere. "There's something I need to tell you." He fidgeted for a second. "Well, something I need to ask you first, actually."

Krystal's eyebrows rose. "Okay."

Bamo reached into his back pocket. He pulled out the tattered, worn wallet his Aunty Aicha had given him years ago after his mother died. He pulled out his mother's necklace, his hands trembling slightly as he fingered it.

Krystal looked down at it and looked up at him. "Bamo, what is it?"

"This was my mother's. It was given to her by her mother before she died, and she had received it from her mother. It was passed down in my family for more than one hundred years."

Krystal gasped and put a hand on her chest.

Bamo looked up from the necklace at Krystal. "My mother was

the most important person in my life, but now that's who you've become to me." He paused but only to clear this throat because he was sure of his decision. "Krystal, I want you to marry me."

Tears filled her eyes. She nodded, too choked up to speak. The yes was in her eyes.

Joy and relief filled Bamo's chest. He put the chain around her neck. "Now this is yours. Ours. When we have our first child, at the right time, you'll give it to her."

Krystal nodded and fingered the necklace. She looked down at it and looked back up at Bamo. He took a few moments to explain about the lion and the bull and what they meant.

Krystal leaned over to kiss him. "I'll treasure it forever. Thank you."

He pulled her into his arms. She had said yes. She was going to be his forever. He hoped in the same country.

"Krystal, there's something else." Bamo let out a deep breath. The first part had actually been easier than what he was about to say. "I don't know quite how to tell you or how to ask you but... lately I've been thinking a lot... and I'm not sure how it would work but..."

"We're moving to Ivory Coast?"

"Wha...How did you..."

Krystal laughed. "Bamo, you're still surprised? You know I know you. Sometimes better than you know yourself. I've been waiting for this. I'm ready. I'm ready to move to your home with you. Like I always tell you, we're going to change the world."

Bamo pulled her into his arms again. Joy and relief filled him to overflowing. "Yes, we are, Krystal. Yes, we are."

PART III

Home Again in Oume

Chapter 20

⧢

Bamo squeezed Krystal's hand. She looked over at him and smiled. After more than twenty hours of flying with a stop in Paris, France, the flight attendant had just announced that they were about to land in Abidjan on the Ivory Coast.

It was a moment for Bamo. He remembered how he had taken this exact journey in reverse, twelve years ago at the tender age of fourteen. His life had taken some incredible twists and turns since then and now he had come full circle. He was coming home to the Ivory Coast. He was equipped with the tools needed to make his home a better place, and with a fiancée who would be his partner in making his lifelong dream come true. God had been especially good to him. He had never imagined he would return so soon and with so much to give.

He couldn't wait to get to Oume to see his mother's school. They had finished building it two years ago and had two full-time teachers with college degrees who were staffing it. His mother's friend, Aicha, had gone to university and had her Master of Education degree. She had taught for a few years in Abidjan, but as soon as they finished building Diaka's school, she came home to be the principal. They also had visiting missionary teachers rotating through. Children from Oume were being educated. They had books and even computers to aid their education.

Their clean water program had been operational for three years now. The farming and irrigation systems were constantly being upgraded. There were Emory students and students from universities all over the US that came over to help with each of the programs.

Chief Noumoury told him of their struggle to maintain their way of life in Oume while accommodating all the improvements. Bamo could understand. He had the sweetest memories of his beautiful, simple life in Oume. He wanted that to remain unspoiled, but he wasn't sure how that could happen in the face of progress.

All that was left of what they had dreamed so far were the levy project and the medical clinic. Bamo felt it would be better to be on the ground for those two. The budgets were large, and he needed them to operate in excellence, so they required close oversight. Bamo's heart soared as he thought of his and the surrounding villages having access to good medical care, because even though the traditional doctors' ways helped, there was only so much herbs could do.

His thoughts moved on to the levy project. The thought of no more lives being lost to flooding was just...

"What are you thinking of so deeply?" Krystal nudged him with her elbow.

"Huh?"

"You keep letting out these long, deep sighs. What are you thinking about?"

"Everything we're going to do." Bamo squeezed Krystal's hand again. "Thanks for the way you've believed in me and encouraged me over the years. Nothing that's happened would have happened if it wasn't for you."

"That's not true. It would have."

"No, it wouldn't have. I'm not sure I would have believed we could do this much this fast." He raised Krystal's hands to his lips and kissed it. "The way you pushed me to believe was...everything. Everything that's happened in Oume is because of you. Thank you."

"Thank God. And you're welcome. And I love you too."

Bamo blushed. By far, Krystal was the greatest gift God had

given him. They were planning a big wedding in Oume. Bamo couldn't believe Krystal had agreed to marry in Ivory Coast, but he understood, the place had become home in her heart since Build Oume was conceived.

As if she'd read his mind, she said, "I finally get to go to Oume. I'll be able to see it with my own eyes."

"I hope it's everything you're expecting. I keep telling you. It's...underdeveloped. It's not—"

"Bamo, I grew up in Haiti. How can Oume be much different? I'm sure I'll love it," she reassured him.

He leaned over and kissed her cheek. "I hope so."

As much as Krystal reassured him that she had grown up on the mission field and could survive in any conditions, he didn't think she could live in Oume. To be honest, after living for twelve years in America, he wasn't sure he could live in Oume.

Besides, with all the work they needed to do, they needed good electricity and decent Internet. Bamo himself didn't think he could go back to life without hot showers every day. This is why they planned to settle in Abidjan with prolonged visits to Oume as needed.

Aunt Namassa had been working hard to prepare for their arrival. She had found a nice duplex for them in the city. One half of it would be their residence and the other half the headquarters for Build Oume. They had already shipped over nice furniture and decorations for the house and office furniture and equipment for their nonprofit. Bamo hoped everything was to Krystal's satisfaction. He really wanted her to be happy with their life there.

"Madames and Monsieurs..."

As the air hostess announced in French and English that they were to land soon, Bamo and Krystal fastened their seatbelts. Bamo's heart began to beat wildly in his chest. He was home!

He hadn't wanted much fanfare at the airport. It took several phone calls and much begging to persuade Chief Noumoury not to meet him at the airport with the entire village in tow. Bamo knew that was the custom and he was sure his father chief was slightly offended at not being allowed to come, but he didn't want Krystal overwhelmed. He could only imagine what it would be like to be met at the airport by fifty villagers hugging and grabbing them, and singing and speaking loud, fast Mandingo. As much as he wanted to see them as soon as he landed, after twenty hours of flying, he thought that would be too much for Krystal.

Aunt Namassa and Uncle Solo would meet them at the airport and take them to their new home. They would rest and then the next day, be ready to head to Oume. The only way Bamo had convinced Chief and Mama Gnale was to say that he wanted them there in Oume making the preparations for his first arrival home after all those years. If they came to get him at the airport, they wouldn't be ready to receive him and his fiancée in the village. He wanted the biggest celebration.

He had sent money ahead to Chief's assistant. He knew they would overdo it and so he wanted to make sure his homecoming cost them nothing.

The plane landed. They exited down descending steps. Bamo dropped his carryon bag and knelt down on the ground. He kissed the concrete and bowed his head, whispering a prayer. "Lord, thank you for bringing me home. Thank you for all I've been able to do for my people and my country, but please bless us to do so much more. Please, Lord, let Krystal be happy here."

When he saw Aunty Namassa, he couldn't believe how much she looked the same. And how much she looked like his mother. He embraced her and cried into her neck. She kept chanting his name over and over. "Bamo, Bamo, Bamo is home." She sang a small song, "Diaka, your son has come home. Are you watching from heaven? Your son has come home."

Bamo shook hands with Uncle Solo and then introduced Krystal. Aunt Namassa hugged her singing, "My daughter, my daughter. You've come home. Diaka, you see your daughter? You see your beautiful daughter? Diaka, we are celebrating together—you in heaven, me on earth. Your son and daughter have come home!"

Aunt Namassa kept singing, dancing, and crying which made

Krystal cry and then Bamo started shedding tears. His heart was bursting.

The whole ride to their new home, Aunt Namassa and Uncle Solo gave them a small tour of Abidjan. Bamo hadn't spent much time there before leaving and had been gone for so many years that it was like introducing him to a whole new world. Everything looked foreign to him. He imagined even more so for Krystal. They looked wide-eyed out of the windows the whole way home.

Bamo realized it was going to take some time for them to learn the city. Fortunately, he had shipped a Toyota Land Cruiser over in one of their many shipments. He bought the SUV to manage their trips to Oume in areas where the road was particularly bad.

When they arrived home, Bamo felt grateful for Aunt Namassa's hard work. The duplex was in a nice neighborhood with good trees and good roads. It was a two-story unit with a nice-sized parlor and kitchen on the main floor and then three bedrooms upstairs. Aunt Namassa had already had the furniture arranged and the curtains hung.

Krystal had agreed to tone down her bright color theme. She said it was fine for her living alone as a woman, but she didn't expect Bamo to live in a pink and yellow house. They had shipped over an earthy green couch and armchair set with brown and crème accents. The ivory-colored curtains made the parlor look fancy.

They toured the whole house. Bamo was especially happy to see the hot water heater off the master bathroom. Hot water—that's what mattered to him most of all.

Bamo watched Krystal taking it all in. She seemed pleased. He was sure she would want to rearrange some things to suit her own taste, but the gleam in her eye made him know she would be okay living here. He let out a deep sigh of relief. It was important to him for her to be happy. He couldn't live his dream here if she wasn't just as happy.

She hugged Aunt Namassa. "Thanks so much for finding this place for us and for arranging everything. I thought I would have so much work to do, but you've taken care of everything. Thanks for that."

Aunt Namassa waved her thanks away. "Anything for my son and daughter. Anything for Diaka's children."

They toured the nonprofit offices next. The parlor was a large conference space with a large, mahogany wood table with nice padded chairs. Stephanie had found the set at an estate sale in an upscale neighborhood and bought it for a cheap price.

Two of the bedrooms were office spaces for him and Krystal, although he knew they'd hardly work in separate rooms. They were used to working in close space. The third bedroom was set up as a guest bedroom for visiting missionaries. He expected to have many.

Aunt Namassa's cell phone rang as they were headed back over to their home. Her smile widened. "We're waiting for you. Come to the house now. Hurry because they need to rest after their long flight."

Bamo gave her a curious look. "Is someone coming?"

Aunt Namassa shooed him into the house. She entered behind him, holding Krystal's hand. "I prepared dinner for you people. I also bought some food. Let me show you your kitchen, my dear. I'll be showing you how to cook Ivorian food while you're staying with me. You have much to learn."

Krystal beamed. "I'm grateful to have a teacher."

It was completely improper for them to live together before they were married, so she would be staying with Aunt Namassa until the wedding. It was to take place in one month's time.

Bamo smiled. Krystal loved to cook, especially things she knew Bamo loved to eat. The thought of her being able to cook attieke or stewed chicken made him smile. He would look for a girl in the village to bring back with them to be house help though. Krystal was here to co-lead Build Oume not to be in the kitchen for hours every day.

When the doorbell rang half an hour later, Krystal and Aunt Namassa were still in the kitchen and Bamo and Uncle Solo were in the parlor drinking a cold Fanta, discussing the latest in politics in the Ivory Coast and Premier League football. Aunt Namassa came rushing down the corridor to the front door.

A few minutes later, she led two men whose faces were identical to each other into the parlor. Bamo jumped up from his chair.

"Bamo, these are your uncles, Baba and Morris. Do you remember—"

"Of course, I remember my mother's brothers." He crossed the room in two steps and embraced them both. They clapped him on the back and hugged.

"Look how our son has grown." Both uncles surveyed him with pride. They looked around the house. "And he's done well for himself."

Bamo introduced Krystal, and they all sat in the parlor, drinking, eating yam with gumbo sauce and talking.

Uncle Baba was a dollar van attendant and Uncle Morris was a warehouse distributor. Bamo knew their lives must have been full of hard work and struggle as they both looked older than he knew them to be. His heart ached to be able to help his uncles' and their families' lives become better.

After they had done all their catching up, Bamo looked around the room at his family. Aunt Namassa had come to visit him over the years in Oume many times. She always asked if he wanted to come back to Abidjan to live with her, but he always refused, never wanting to leave Oume. His uncles hadn't been a major part of his life. Each time they saw him, they were loving and gentle and told him stories of their mother. They never once invited him to come live with them in Abidjan.

As they were all talking and laughing and enjoying being reunited, Bamo couldn't help but wonder why. Family was a big priority in his country, and it was unusual for family to let a child be raised by someone else. Maybe Aunt Namassa had always told them that Bamo didn't want to come home and preferred to live in Oume. Maybe they never had enough money to support him.

From the way they were dressed and the way they had described their lives now, it seemed as if they were still struggling.

Looking at his uncles, Bamo pondered for a moment what his life would have been like if he had moved to Abidjan with this family. Bamo wondered if God had worked it out for him to be born and raised in Oume to end up in America with Stephanie and Jason so he could come back and bring change. He looked over at Krystal. He was silently grateful for the way God had directed his life.

"What of your father—my grandfather? Is he well?"

Baba and Morris shifted in their seats. Aunt Namassa looked down at the floor.

Bamo frowned. For his whole childhood, he had asked the same question and the reaction was almost always the same. The man never came to visit him in Oume, and Bamo had never been brought to the house to see him. He had never met the man. Once, he asked if his grandfather was dead and he was told his grandfather was very much alive. The subject was changed, and that was the end of the conversation.

"Is he still living?" Bamo insisted. He was a man now. No longer a child. He expected answers. He knew they could tell by his tone. He was respectful, but firmer than he could have ever been as a child.

"He's still living," Baba said and looked at Morris. Morris looked at Aunt Namassa who looked at Uncle Solo.

"Can I go and see him?" Bamo asked. He had asked several times as a child and there was always some excuse that didn't make sense, even to his young mind.

The room was quiet for a while. Finally, Morris spoke. "He's very ill. It's not a good time to see him. When he's better, we can talk about it."

"Very ill? Not a good time to see him? Talk about it when he's better?" Bamo felt himself getting a bit angry. "I don't understand. Do you all realize I've never met my mother's father? My mother is not on this earth anymore, but the man who gave birth to her is here. I've never seen him. I've never laid eyes on him. This is not acceptable to me anymore. And if he's ill, shouldn't I at least meet him before he dies?"

Bamo looked around the room at all of his silent relatives. He could see traces of his mother in Aunt Namassa and his uncles. Shouldn't he be allowed to see her in his grandfather?

"It's late and you people should be very tired. We should be going so you can rest." Aunt Namassa stood and Uncle Solo followed her. "I promise, Bamo, after you've rested, we'll have a long talk about taking you to see your grandfather. You'll have to be patient with me, okay? But you have my word."

"Aunt Namassa—"

"Bamo..." Krystal squeezed his leg. "Let's get some rest as she said. Your aunt has given her word. Okay?"

Bamo nodded. His uncles stood. The sweetness of the reunion with his family had soured a little, but Bamo was determined to fix it.

"Krystal and I will travel to Oume for a visit. Then we'll be back in Abidjan. Maybe you both can show me around some?"

Baba and Morris both smiled. "We'd love to show you around, nephew. Just call us when you return," Baba said, and Morris nodded.

"Aunt Namassa, you'll let Krystal sleep late tomorrow? We lost a lot of hours on the plane and then the time zone change. Let her sleep as long as she can tomorrow. Maybe the cooking lessons can wait until we get back from Oume."

"Bamo, I know how to take care of your wife. Are you telling me—a grown woman—how to care for another woman? Your fiancée will be safe with me. Can a man care for a woman better than me? Ha! This Bamo has traveled and thinks he knows a woman's ways."

Bamo laughed. "Okay, Aunty. Sorry now. Please forgive me. I know you'll care for her well."

"Don't ever doubt me, my son."

Bamo ushered them to the car. He held Krystal's hand. "You'll be fine without me?"

He didn't feel right bringing her to a whole different country and then leaving her alone. He knew Aunt Namassa would indeed take good care of her, but she had to be overwhelmed with being in this brand new environment. He wanted to be with her so she would be comfortable.

There were so many old ways here. It wouldn't be proper for her to stay with him in the house with them not being married, and there was no way in the world he could leave her alone in the house. It was the tradition that she would stay with his mother, in this case, Aunt Namassa until they were married. Bamo had gone over it a million times in his head, but he knew going with Aunt Namassa was the only way.

"Bamo, you worry too much. I'll be fine with your family. Your aunt loves me already. She's promised to take good care of me." Krystal squeezed his hand. "Please stop worrying about me. I'm fine."

He stroked her cheek.

"I should have taken you to visit my home where I grew up in Haiti. Then you'd stop fussing and worrying about me."

Bamo had gone to meet Krystal's parents in Oklahoma not long after he proposed. He had asked her father for her hand in marriage and had taken gifts to her family, as he would have if he had been meeting his in-laws for the first time in Africa.

Krystal brushed her lips against his cheek. "Go inside and get some rest. Try not to worry. I'll see you tomorrow, okay?"

Bamo couldn't kiss her good night in front of his family. He settled for a hug. "Okay, rest well. I'll see you in the afternoon and then the next morning, we leave for Oume."

"I can't wait."

"Me either."

Bamo was anxious to take Krystal to his childhood home.

Chapter 21

Bamo was fidgeting nervously in the car. They were two hours into their trip to Oume. The closer they got, the more nervous he was. Would it be as beautiful as he remembered? Would the people be happy to see him? Would Krystal be okay there?

He looked over at her in the seat next to him. She seemed very happy so far. She and Aunt Namassa were getting along better than he had expected. She had come to the house with some beef stew in gravy with some white rice and yam they had made together. She was so excited to have cooked an Ivorian meal and couldn't wait to learn others.

Aunt Namassa and Uncle Solo were in the back seat. They wanted to be there for Bamo's welcome home celebration. His uncles would come for the wedding.

The further they got from the city, the more trees they saw and the fresher the air became. The sky was a huge, vast sea of blue before them and the pristinely white clouds hung low. This was the sky he remembered—expansive and majestic—always reminding him that God and his mother were watching from above.

About five minutes from the edge of the village, Bamo slowed down. The streets were lined with children. He knew the whole village knew he was coming. He came to a stop and rolled down the window.

"Are you Mr. Bamo?" a young boy of about seven years asked.

"Yes, sir. I am."

The boy smiled a toothy grin and screamed, "It's Mr. Bamo," to the rest of the children. They jumped and sang and gathered around the car until Bamo couldn't drive anymore. He got out of the car, and they surrounded him, all trying to hug and touch him.

"Thank you for our school, Mr. Bamo. I can read!"

Other children joined the small girl in shouting their thanks for the school. Some chanted their ABC's and counted. Others did their times table and spelled words. Bamo laughed as he hugged them and patted them on their backs. Krystal joined him outside the car, her eyes full of joy and excitement.

The kids swarmed them for another five minutes until Aunt Namassa came out of the car. "You children run ahead now. Let us come. Go and tell Chief his son Bamo is here!"

The children all took off running for the village after being reminded of the reason they had been sent out to the road. Bamo and Krystal got back in the car and drove slowly behind the children into Oume.

When they got to the edge of the village, they couldn't drive anymore. The road was flooded with people. Bamo wondered whether anyone had gone to the farm that day or had they all stayed at home, waiting for his arrival. The thought caused his heart to swell.

"Bamo!"

Bamo turned toward the direction of the female voice screaming his name. He saw his mother's friend, Aunt Aicha running toward him. He ran toward her and embraced her. Tears streamed down her face.

"Diaka's Bamo! Look at you. You're a grown man. A beautiful, grown man."

"Aunty Aicha, I'm so happy to see you."

"Come to the Baobab tree. Everyone is waiting for you there."

Bamo left the keys with Uncle Solo to bring the car into the village. He took Krystal's hand, and they followed Aicha to the village tree. People were swarming around them, reaching out to touch him, calling his name. A group of women on the side of the road were singing a song to welcome him and dancing. Krystal was taking it all in, eyes wide in wonder, drinking in such an experience. Bamo's eyes were filled with love. He was being welcomed home to his Oume.

As he reached the tree, he saw his mothers all there, lining the path to the tree. All the women he had lived with as a child were there, except for Mama Kady, who had died of malaria a few years back. He hugged each one of them, tears on his cheeks mixing with the tears on theirs.

When he reached the tree, Chief Noumoury and Mama Gnale were waiting there. Mama Gnale pulled him into an embrace and wept and wept. Bamo was overcome with tears.

"Gnale, leave the boy. You'll soak him with tears." Chief patted her on the back while she was still holding Bamo.

"Where do you see a boy? Our Bamo is a man. He's a man." She pulled back from the hug and looked up at Bamo, at least a foot taller than she. She stepped back.

Chief Noumoury and Bamo stood face to face.

"My son, have you come home?"

"Yes, Father, I have come."

"You've kept your promise? You did everything our God took you to America to do?"

"Yes, Father. I've kept my promise. God has done more than we expected and now I've come home."

"Then welcome home, my son." Chief Noumoury pulled Bamo into an embrace. Bamo tried to be a big man and not cry, but the moment was too much. He had last embraced his father chief as a boy and now they were standing chest to chest, hugging as men. Bamo had kept his promise and was a man that his father could be proud of.

The people around them cheered and sang as they hugged. Men usually didn't show long displays of affection, but the situation called for it.

When he had finished greeting the chief, Bamo looked around for Krystal. She was right by his side, her cheeks damp with tears and her eyes full of joy and love. Bamo introduced her to every-one. They all greeted her—some with polite handshakes, others called her daughter and pulled her into an embrace. The love of his Oume family for her was real.

Bamo showed Krystal the tree where so many things had occurred in childhood. His birth celebration, his mother's funeral, his departure celebration and every other occasion in the village. This place was the center of his memories in Oume. Krystal looked at the tree and looked at him. The look in her eyes said she understood how significant it was to him.

After he promised to come to his father chief's house in about an hour, Bamo led Krystal to the house he had grown up in, right across from the clearing that held the Baobab tree. Uncle Solo and Aunt Namassa had pulled the car up to the house and had already walked to the chief's palace.

Bamo led Krystal into the little two-room clay hut, showing her their main room and then the little bedroom he had shared with his mother. He took her back to the outdoor kitchen. Someone had kept the house well swept and cleaned. He could tell that a new mattress had been put there for his arrival.

"How can a house made of mud still be standing after all these years?" Krystal asked as she moved around the house, touching the mud walls.

Bamo laughed. "I don't know how, but these houses can last forever. We could leave it to our grandchildren if we wanted to."

As Bamo walked through the house, his soul was flooded with memories of his life with his mother there. He had left the house when she died to live with all his mothers in the village and finally with Chief Noumoury and Mama Gnale. Aunty Aicha had moved into the house when her father remarried.

Every space in the house held a memory. He could see his mother sweeping the parlor every morning while singing a song her mother used to sing to her. He could see them lying in the bed at night and her finally getting him his own mattress when he got old enough to be too big to sleep with her. Every night, she would tell him stories until he fell asleep. He could see her out in the kitchen, cooking and singing, preparing meals for him with so much love. He missed her so much. His heart swelled.

Aicha walked in from the courtyard. "Not a day goes by that I don't think about her."

Bamo looked at her and nodded.

"What you've done with the school is beautiful. I know Mama Diaka is happy looking down from heaven and so proud of the man you've become. Bamo, you've made her happy, and you've served her memory well."

Except for the day he left Oume and the day of his mother's funeral, Bamo couldn't remember a day he had shed so many tears. He was glad the tears he was crying today were tears of joy.

Krystal was somehow giving him space and being there for him at the same time, squeezing his hand, rubbing his back, being loving and comforting in the way she always was.

After they spent some time at his house, Bamo and Krystal walked to the chief's house. Everywhere they went, they were surrounded by young girls looking at Krystal and children talking to Bamo. The young girls kept touching Krystal's hair and looking at her clothes. She was like a celebrity from America to them.

Bamo was flooded with more happy memories when he entered the chief's palace. He, Krystal, Aunt Namassa and Uncle Solo and his aunt's friend, Poupette, and her husband Kaba who had initially brought his mother to the village all gathered around the chief's large table for a meal. Mama Gnale and all of Bamo's mothers had made a buffet of alloko, attieke, fried fish, yam, oxtail stew, beef stew, white rice, couscous, spinach stew, okra soup, and all kind of fruit from the village. They all laughed and talked. Bamo leaned over to translate the parts of the conversation spoken in Mandingo to Krystal. She seemed happy to just take it all in.

When dinner was over, Bamo and Krystal were exhausted. They still hadn't fully recovered from jetlag and the day had been an emotional one.

Bamo handed Krystal over to Mama Gnale, who would be hosting her in the chief's palace. Just as he was turning to leave, the drums started beating.

"What is that?" Krystal asked.

Bamo smiled. "They send messages to the neighboring villages with drums. They're telling everyone of the celebration tomorrow. They're telling everyone that their son Bamo is home. Sleep well. Tomorrow will be busy."

He walked Aunt Namassa and Uncle Solo to Poupette and Kaba's house where they would sleep. Finally, he ended up at the center of the village at his mother's house. His home that had been waiting on him, that was always his. He said good night to the Baobab tree and went to bed, dreaming of his mother the whole night.

◦◦◦

The next morning, Bamo heard the hum of the village waking up at 5 a.m. He knew the women were in their kitchens making rice pudding and handmade bread for the celebration day breakfast. His mouth was happy as he remembered the taste.

He got up and went to the chief's house to go look for Krystal, only to find that Aicha has already come for her. He was directed to Aicha's new house where she lived with her husband and children and found them in the kitchen. He couldn't believe Aicha had Krystal stirring rice pudding over a three-stone fire. The sight of his wife-to-be cooking over the large fire pot made him chuckle. Aunt Namassa and now Aicha were determined to make her into an Ivorian woman.

The two communicated easily in French and were chatting away about everything under the sun.

By 7:30, the area around the Baobab tree was filled with people eating breakfast and talking. By the time Bamo and Krystal reached, there were at least two hundred people there plus the usual cows, chickens, and goats meandering around the people.

About a half hour later, the drum started beating, announcing the arrival of the chief and his staff. Women, dressed in beautiful African dresses, lined the edge of the clearing area, singing and doing traditional dances.

The chief and his staff, accompanied by their wives, proceeded to the main area of the clearing where their tables had been set up. All of Bamo's mothers followed. Everyone was dressed in beautiful, colorful traditional African fabrics.

Bamo watched Krystal taking in the whole scene with a look of awe on her face.

When everyone was in place, the drum stopped beating, and the village messenger announced, "Ladies and gentlemen, here is Chief Noumoury."

Chief Noumoury stood and greeted the crowd. "Dear residents, it is my deepest pleasure to tell all of Oume and the world that my son, Bamo, has returned home."

The whole village and guests from the surrounding villages applauded loudly and cheered.

The chief welcomed Bamo to the stage. He grabbed Krystal's hand and led her up there with him.

The chief continued, "My son became a man of trust. He left here with everyone's blessing twelve years ago. Even though his life in America was good—truly blessed by God, he never forgot us. We all know of the great things he has done for this village. He worked hard and has helped us to have clean water, has helped our farms and has continued his mother's legacy by building the school she always dreamed of."

He paused as the people cheered. "And if that wasn't enough, he has come home to do even more. He has come to build a good clinic to improve our health. And..." Chief paused. "He will help to build levies to prevent the floods that took the lives of his mother, Diaka, and my own father many years ago. We all have lost people due to flooding and now, that tragedy of our lives will come to an end."

Chief paused again as the people applauded, this time more solemnly.

"I want to give him the opportunity to greet you. And to introduce a very special person that he's brought to visit us."

Bamo stood, waiting for the people to stop cheering, clapping and singing so he could speak. When he tried to speak, he was overwhelmed with emotion.

He finally addressed the crowd. "People of Oume, mothers, fathers, brothers, sisters, aunts, uncles and all residents. I'm back home." Cheers erupted again.

"I am grateful to stand before you as a son of this village. If there's anything I've done for Oume, it's because of the way you welcomed my mother in her worst time. You gave her, and then me, a wonderful life here in your village. And then when she died, you continued to love me and care for me. Everything I've done and will do for Oume is only a small way of saying thanks for the life you've given me."

The people cheered and shouted his name. "Bamo!! Bamo!! Bamo!!"

"And thank you for your warm welcome to me and my fiancée. Her name is Krystal. She has stood by my side in everything that's been done here in Oume. And now she's come home to Ivory Coast. We are here to do great things to build Oume. We will do it with you and with God's help and blessing. Thank you."

The people cheered and sang. The women at the edge of the clearing danced. The program ended, and the people began to eat the large feast that had been prepared for the day. The people ate and talked. The children ran around and kept coming up to greet Bamo and Krystal.

Bamo had sent money ahead to Mama Gnale and her staff for a huge feast for the whole village. They had seasoned meat and vegetable sauce, baked yams, white and seasoned rice with some stew goat and lamb meat, fish stew, rice pudding with some fresh traditional bread, some fresh milk from the village cow, and lots of fruit grown right there in the village.

After they ate, the chief and his staff gave Bamo and Krystal a tour of the improvements that had been made in the village. Bamo cried as he walked through his mother's school. He was sure it was more than anything she could have ever dreamed.

They were shown the city's water system. They drove the SUV to one of the farms to see the new irrigation system and then drove through a large area with many farms to see how they were prospering.

Bamo and Krystal had seen pictures of everything, but it was overwhelming to see all they had accomplished in person. Everywhere they went, people expressed gratitude for all the good they had done over the past five years. They flooded them with bags of fruits and vegetables they had grown. "These are expensive in the city. We'll make sure we send you food every week."

By the time the sun was starting to set, they were again filled with happy exhaustion. Before dropping her off at the chief's house, Bamo asked Krystal to come to his mother's hut. He had invited Aunt Namassa and Uncle Solo there for a drink before they went to sleep.

They reflected on the day for a little while until Bamo finally got up the courage to say what he really wanted to say.

"Aunt Namassa, why have I never met my grandfather?"

The house was so silent the crickets, frogs, and birds could all be heard singing outside.

Uncle Solo put his hand on Aunt Namassa's leg. They shared a look. She let out a deep breath.

"Bamo, there are things you don't know about your past. Your mother's past. And some things are left better that way."

"Aunty, you know I respect you, but I don't agree. I've never met my mother's father, but the man is alive and breathing, in this same country, in the city where I'm about to live. My dear mother's father. All my life, you've kept me from him. I want to know why. I'm a man. Whatever you need to tell me, I can handle it."

"Please, Bamo, if you'll just give me time, I'll tell you everything. Please, Bamo, out of respect for your grandfather, please give me a chance to put some things in order before I take you to meet him."

Bamo's heart quickened. "You'll take me to meet him?"

Aunt Namassa let out a measured breath. "Yes," she said tentatively at first, but then more firmly. "Yes. But at first, I'll just introduce you as a visitor from the US."

Bamo frowned. "But—"

Aunt Namassa held up her hand. "Please, Bamo, allow me to arrange the situation first. But I promise you'll meet him. I've said it before and I'll say it again, you have my word."

Bamo was silent. For now, that would have to do.

Chapter 22

They spent three more days in Oume, Bamo showing Krystal all his favorite places and introducing her to and spending time with each of the mothers that raised him. They spent time with Chief and Mama Gnale and spent time in Diaka's school with Aicha. The time seemed to fly by. They returned to Abidjan.

Krystal rearranged things in the house to her taste. Aunt Namassa took her to the big market in the middle of the city and also to some more expensive shops in the mall to buy simple decorations that would make their house more like home.

She seemed to enjoy spending time with Aunt Namassa, cooking and shopping in the market. She was adjusting much better and much faster than Bamo had expected her to, and it made him happy. It made him more comfortable with his decision to move her to Ivory Coast.

Aunt Namassa kept her promise and a few days after they returned to Abidjan, Bamo was literally shaking as they arrived at the compound where his mother spent the first part of her life.

His mother, Diaka, had told him stories many nights before he slept of her life in Abidjan. As he was thinking back, he realized those stories always honored her father and the memory of her mother. But every time he asked whether his grandfather had also died, his mother said nothing. Her eyes would cloud and her mouth would become a tight line and she would only say that her father had loved her mother and she and her brothers deeply and had been a very good father. She never said anything more than that.

Remembering that and Aunt Namassa stressing to him again that he would be introduced as a friend rather than as a grandson made Bamo's mind fill with questions.

As they entered the house, Bamo's uncles greeted him. They had agreed with Aunt Namassa that Bamo should meet his grandfather. There was a certain tension in the air that made Bamo wonder all the more what had really happened that made his mother move to Oume in the first place.

The smell of sickness filled the air. Krystal held his hand tighter.

"Do you want to wait in the car?" Bamo asked her.

She pressed her lips together and shook her head.

Baba gestured to a seat in the small parlor. "Please be comfortable. Our father is in the room. He's very sick. Let me go make sure it's okay for you to come inside."

Bamo looked around the small house.

Morris spoke up. "Your mother rented this house for us when she started her job. Many of the things here are things she bought, if you can believe it." He stood and went in the same direction Uncle Baba had gone.

Bamo could believe it. Everything looked old and worn, like it could fall apart at any moment. He looked at Aunt Namassa with questions in his eyes. If he had known his grandfather was living like this, he would have sent money. Why hadn't she told him that his mother's father was living in such poverty and was sick and needed help?

As if she understood the question in his eyes as he scanned the room, Aunt Namassa said, "Your grandfather is a very proud man, Bamo. After your mother left here, he hasn't been willing to accept my help for anything. I think he may have thought it came from her. He doesn't even know she's..." Aunt Namassa's voice trailed off.

She held up her hand before he could speak. "Please, Bamo. I promise I'll tell you everything very soon."

Uncle Baba came out of the room and nodded to Bamo. Bamo's feet felt like lead as he walked into his grandfather's bedroom. The smell grew stronger. He motioned for Krystal to wait for him in the parlor. She seemed grateful.

Bamo walked over to the bed. His grandfather looked sickly thin, his cheeks sunken in. His eyes were tightly closed as if he were in pain.

"What's wrong with him?" Bamo whispered to Uncle Baba.

Baba whispered back, "The traditional doctor says he has a parasite. He's using herbs to try to flush them out."

"Traditional doctor? Herbs?" Bamo's whisper was so loud he might as well be talking.

"The hospital is too expensive."

Bamo frowned. Baba shrugged.

"Please get him ready. We're taking him to a hospital. Now." He didn't want to speak disrespectfully to his uncle, but he added a firmness to his voice that wouldn't allow for an argument.

Thirty minutes later, Baba and Morris had washed their father and dressed him in fresh, clean clothes that hung loosely from his thin frame. Bamo thought that if those were the clothes he used to wear, this illness had caused him to lose a lot of weight.

They carried him gently out to the car. As instructed, Morris drove them to the best hospital in Abidjan. It took hours, but Grandpa Moussa—as Bamo's uncles called his grandfather—was finally admitted to the hospital. Bamo and Uncle Baba sat in the hospital. Bamo had instructed his Uncle Morris to take Krystal and Aunt Namassa home.

The doctors finally sent them home, saying they were still waiting for the results of tests and would know more in the morning. Uncle Morris came back with the truck. Bamo finally went home, exhausted from all the emotions of the day and the long wait in the hospital.

Baba and Morris were relieved when the doctors told them their father was very ill, but would recover with good treatment. Bamo wondered if they had just planned to keep their father at home until he died. He didn't at all understand what they had been thinking but kept his thoughts to himself.

The next day, Bamo decided not to go to the hospital. Being around his grandfather and his uncles was only making him wonder all the more about his past. Nobody was forthcoming with the truth, and it really bothered him. He asked Baba to keep him updated with phone calls but decided to stay home and work.

Krystal came over from Aunt Namassa's and they started putting things in order to get the NGO—the Ivory Coast arm of their US nonprofit—off the ground. They worked for a few hours before the call came from Baba. He explained what the doctors had found. His grandfather had a bad infection in his intestines that had spread to his blood. If he had stayed home a few days longer, he would have died. The doctors were calling it fortuitous that Bamo had brought him to the hospital.

Bamo was angry by the time he hung up, even though Baba had thanked him profusely over and over for saving his father's life. Bamo didn't ask him why they hadn't taken him to the hospital. He couldn't imagine any logical answer for why they would have allowed him to die at home. Was his grandfather that proud?

When they started working again, Bamo snapped at Krystal about something that wasn't important. She stood up from the large table in the parlor of the work section of their duplex and came over to where he was sitting. She took the pen out of his hand and laid it on the table.

"Bamo, I don't understand what's happening with your family, and I know this isn't easy for you."

He pulled his chair back from the table and pulled Krystal onto his lap. "I'm sorry. You don't ever deserve me talking to you that way. Please forgive me."

She wrapped her arms around his neck. "I forgive you and I love you. Please, try not to be so upset about it. We both know that whatever happened between your mother and her father must have been bad. Promise me you'll not let it affect you. I understand you want to know, but whatever happened led you to the life you have now. The life you and I have together. No matter how bad it was, it led you to me. You can't regret that, can you?"

Bamo pressed his head into Krystal's chest. She was right. Whatever had happened between his grandfather and his mother had brought the most beautiful woman into his life. He hadn't ended up like his uncles. Whatever it was had given him the gift his life was now. Even before he found out the truth, he forgave.

Krystal kissed his forehead. "I love you, Bamo. Let me feed you. Do you want some attieke or alloko with fried tilapia?

He lifted his head and gave her a questioning look. "You know how to make all those dishes?"

"Of course. Aunt Namassa taught me. I'm preparing to be the best wife ever." She stood and walked toward the kitchen.

His eyes followed her to the kitchen. "You're already so much more..." He whispered under his breath.

Bamo made some phone calls. He was setting up meetings with some of the contractors he had contacted while still in the US about building the levies. He also talked to some contractors about the medical clinic. He let them know he was now in the country and planned to set up meetings in a few weeks. As much as he was ready to start working on their projects, he still wanted to give he and Krystal a chance to settle in, rest some more, and get used to their new surroundings.

Bamo continued to check on his grandfather by phone. A few days into the hospital admission, Bamo went to see him. Baba led him into the room. Sitting up in bed eating bread and drinking tea, his grandfather already looked much better. The difference was like night and day. Bamo couldn't believe that five days on medicine and fluids in the hospital was the difference between life and death. His grandfather might have died at home for no reason other than no access to healthcare.

"Grandpa Moussa, this is the young man I told you about that brought you to the hospital," Baba said.

Grandpa Moussa put down his teacup and held out his hand. "Young man."

Bamo took tentative steps toward the bed. It was as if his legs didn't want to work. "Sir."

For the first time in his life, he shook hands with his mother's father.

"Thank you so much for bringing me to the hospital. The doctors have scolded me for staying at home. They said you've saved my life. I'm not sure what I've done to deserve your kindness, but I thank you." He pumped Bamo's hand up and down. "I thank you very much, young man."

"You're welcome, sir."

Bamo studied his face. Baba and Morris looked like their father, but his mother had a completely different face. She had told him she looked like her mother, and Aunt Namassa always said the same thing. Diaka looked exactly like their mother, Jeneba.

"Please have a seat, young man. Baba tells me you're here from America. How long will you be visiting?"

Bamo looked at Baba. He wasn't sure what his grandfather had been told. He didn't want to contradict anything his uncles had said.

Baba stepped in. "Father, you'll have time to get to know Bamo soon. Please, you should finish your tea so you can rest. He's just stopping by and has to leave."

Bamo nodded. Baba escorted him out into the hallway. "Thanks again, Bamo. He's doing so much better. The doctors say he should be discharged in a few days. Thank you for everything."

"You don't have to thank me. I'm happy he's fine." He pressed some money into Baba's hand. "Please, you should buy some things for the house. A new mattress and bed linens. Get rid of everything from when he was sick. Later, we should get some furniture for the rest of the house as well."

Baba kept thanking him over and over until Bamo stopped him.

"If you really want to thank me, you'll tell me the truth about everything. Or will I continue being the benevolent young man from America?"

Bamo knew his tone was terse, but he was tired. If they weren't going to tell him the truth and him truly get to meet his grandfather—as a grandson, the son of Diaka—he wasn't sure he wanted to continue spending time around the old man. He didn't like secrets and lies and wasn't willing to continue in the way things were going.

Later that evening, he called Aunt Namassa and gave her the update on his grandfather. She began thanking him and he stopped her. He tried to maintain as much respect as he could in his voice. He didn't want things to be tense around his family when he had just been reunited with them.

The next morning, when Bamo saw Aunt Namassa's number on his phone, he didn't answer. He needed to get his mind together before he had another conversation with her. Deep down, he was angry and didn't want to speak disrespectfully to her. She called three more times, and each time, he let it ring without answering.

A few minutes later, Krystal called. "Bamo, are you still sleeping?"

"I woke up with the sun as always. How are you? Are you okay over there? Should I come and get you?"

"Bamo, I keep telling you I'm fine. Aunt Namassa thinks you're angry with her and you're not answering the phone, so she asked me to call. Your aunt and uncle want to come over. They want to talk to you. About your grandfather."

Bamo took in a deep breath before speaking. "Tell them to come. Tell them I'm ready."

Chapter 23

Bamo leaned back in his chair. He looked at Aunt Namassa and Uncle Solo. Uncle Solo was quiet as usual while Aunt Namassa unraveled the painful story of his mother's past—his past. Her words weighed heavy on his chest and it almost felt like he couldn't breathe. Krystal put a hand on his leg but knew to let him think in peace. What words could she say, anyway?

Bamo leaned over and put his head in his hands as he thought of his mother, pregnant with him and disowned by her father. He thought of her being so depressed that she wanted to die. His heart loved Chief Noumoury and the people of Oume all the more for accepting her in her worst time. A tear spilled down his cheek.

"Mama Diaka..." he murmured.

Uncle Solo cleared his throat. "You have to understand, Bamo. It was tradition. A woman pregnant and unmarried brings great shame upon her family. It was tradition to disown her."

Bamo shook his head.

Aunt Namassa spoke up. "Please try to understand, Bamo. You've lived away from here most of your life. You don't understand traditions and family here."

"You're right. I don't understand. I don't understand how my mother could care for her father and brothers for years and just like that... They just disown her—and me. He couldn't forgive after a few years gone by and take her back in?"

Krystal held his hand. Her touched stopped him from shaking.

He looked at Aunt Namassa. "Does he know anything about me? Does he know how she died?"

Aunt Namassa hung her head. Uncle Solo spoke softly, "No, Bamo."

"After all these years, he's never asked about her? Never asked about me? His own daughter—daughter of his beloved wife whom he loved so much—just ceased to exist for him?"

Aunt Namassa and Uncle Solo were silent. Bamo held his head in his hands.

After a few moments, Uncle Solo spoke. "What happened in the past should stay in the past and because of that past, all that is happening is in fact happening for all our good. Bamo, look at your life now. Even though you may believe your grandfather was wrong, look at how you've turned out."

It was the same thing Krystal had told him. No matter how badly his grandfather had treated his mother and through her, him, he had a wonderful life.

Krystal mouthed the words to him she'd spoken earlier. "No regrets."

Uncle Solo continued, "Bamo, you must forgive your grandfather and concentrate on building a solid and respectful relationship with him and your two uncles. Family is very important."

Bamo wanted with everything inside him to shout that if family was so important, then why had his grandfather disowned his mother? And why had they allowed it to be. But he remembered Krystal's words, no regrets. He squeezed her hand and pulled his emotions back inside his heart. He didn't regret his life in America, and he surely didn't regret her.

"Thank you for telling me the truth. It must not have been easy for you, so I appreciate it." It took all Bamo's strength to be gracious. "I have a lot to think about." He sat silent for a few minutes.

"I guess the other question that comes to my mind is, what of my father? The man that impregnated my mother and then refused to acknowledge me. You say you spoke to him yourself, face-to-face, and he refused to help her and denied the pregnancy? Who is this man? Is he still in Abidjan?"

"I don't know, Bamo. I haven't seen or heard of him since that day in his office. That's a promise." Aunt Namassa held up her hand with a solemn look on her face.

Bamo nodded. "I'm very tired now. Please, I'd like to rest. I'm sure my grandfather will be going home in the next few days. If you need to come, take the truck to bring him from the hospital to his house, let me know. We'll arrange it. I gave Baba some money to get some things for the house. Perhaps you can help him to make some good purchases." Bamo's voice was flat.

"Bamo, please—" Uncle Solo started.

Bamo held up a hand. "I will always treat my grandfather with respect. I will do whatever is needed to help take care of him. I will find it in my heart to forgive. Please, I just need to rest, and I need some time."

Bamo squeezed Krystal's hand and leaned to kiss her cheek. "You want to stay and work? Or just stay and rest? I can take you back later, or I'll stay in the guestroom next door and you can stay in the bedroom here." The sour feeling in Bamo's stomach made him want to keep his fiancée far away from his family, because they no longer felt like family.

"Aunt Namassa and I are going to the market. We're cooking later. And she's going to take me to buy some fabric and then we're going to the tailor to have some dresses made." She put a hand on his cheek. "But I can stay here if you want me to, if you need me to be around."

He shook his head. "I only want to sleep. If you're okay..."

"Bamo, I'm okay. I'm worried that you're not okay."

Bamo shook his head again. He kissed her cheek once more, stood and walked upstairs to the bedroom.

❦

Bamo couldn't shake the negative feelings from the meeting with Uncle Solo and Aunt Namassa. He decided to throw himself into working on Build Oume, especially since he knew the circumstances under which they took him in. He was all the more grateful and all the more committed to helping his village. The village that saved his mother's life and his life.

He started scheduling meetings with contractors for the levies and for the hospital. Krystal asked him to slow down, expressing concern that he was working too hard, too fast, but he kept going. He had to keep apologizing to her for being distant and sullen.

He told her she didn't have to attend the meetings if she didn't want to. He still wanted her to take her time settling in to her new environment. She told him she'd come to some of the meetings, but not all.

A week after he'd been sulking around the house and office, Krystal came behind his chair, wrapped her arms around him and kissed his cheek. "Bamo, how long are you going to stay like this? It isn't good. I keep telling you, your life has been good, in spite of, and in fact, because of your grandfather's actions."

Bamo reached up and wrapped his arms around his fiancée. He knew he was hurting her with the way he was behaving. He was trying to fix his heart, but it wasn't working. He had never been angry like this in his whole life. He wasn't sure what would make it better.

"I'm thankful to God for the way my life turned out. But my grandfather wasn't doing me good on purpose. God just fixed the terrible mistake he made."

"Bamo, I don't like seeing you like this. This isn't who you are."

"Who I am?"

"Right now? Angry, bitter, and resentful. This is not the Bamo I know and love. This is not the man you are. Do whatever you have to do to get the peace back in your heart. This is bad for you."

Bamo pondered her words. He had tried the whole week to find a way to forgive his grandfather and even his uncles. Couldn't they have done something? The more he thought about the situation to try to find a way to forgive, the more angry he became. They had abandoned his mother. They had no idea she would find such love in Oume and it seemed, they didn't care.

He knew Krystal was right. He didn't feel like himself, and he didn't like the dark feeling that had taken over his insides.

Krystal rubbed his arms. Bamo loved her soft, sweet touch. He wished it could go into his heart and chase out all the anger that had settled there.

She spoke softly into his ear, "Aunt Namassa called. She said your grandfather was discharged from the hospital today. They used part of the money you gave to buy his medicines. They were also able to get new things for the house, as you said."

She paused and let out a deep breath. "She said he wants to thank you. He wants to have you and the whole family over for dinner so he can thank you properly in their presence. She's begging for you to find it in your heart to come."

Bamo sat there—silent—absorbing Krystal's touch. He wanted to get lost in it and forget all about these family issues.

She spoke again, "I understand if you don't want to, but I think it would be beautiful if you could find it in your heart to forgive your grandfather. What if God wants to reunite your family after all these years?"

Bamo thought about it. Would his grandfather accept him now? It was one thing for him to be a benevolent stranger, but would his grandfather accept him as a grandson? The son of his disowned daughter, Diaka?

And if he didn't, would Bamo be able to handle it?

Krystal left him alone with his thoughts. She seemed to know how to say exactly what she needed to say and then disappear to let him process.

What could he do to fix his heart? What would it take for him to forgive? He sat for a while thinking and then finally called the one person he knew could help—Chief Noumoury.

After they exchanged pleasantries, Bamo asked with a pained

voice, "Father Chief, did you know about how my mother, Diaka, came to your village? Did you know her situation?"

Bamo knew immediately by the heavy silence that Chief Noumoury knew the whole story. He finally spoke, "My son, why do you ask?"

Bamo let out a deep sigh. "I asked to see my grandfather. After all these years, they finally let me see him. But I had to introduce myself to him as a stranger. A stranger."

Chief Noumoury let out a low groan. "Eh, Bamo, sorry."

"What kind of man does that? How could he treat my mother like that? How could he throw us away like that?" Bamo released the pain he'd been feeling since the visit from Aunt Namassa. He had been choking it down, but couldn't, not anymore. He heaved heavy sobs for what felt like a long time.

While he cried, Chief Noumoury kept saying, "Sorry, Bamo, eh, sorry."

The chief was silent for a few minutes before taking a deep breath. "Bamo, you must know, my son, that you came from a fine recipe created by God. He carefully put all the ingredients together for your life to cause you to become who you are, right now, today. Anything that your mother, your father, your grandfather, your Aunt Namassa, even me—anything that any of us has done was orchestrated by God to create the perfect recipe for who you are today. God works in mysterious ways and only at the end can anyone understand what He knew all along."

Bamo listened silently as the chief continued.

"You are a messenger, my son, chosen to show the world God's goodness and His ability to create greatness in things that didn't seem to begin well. Your story began in pain and struggle and so much difficulty, but it has become a beautiful story that tells the world a powerful message about God.

"Your story is also a message to many. Never abandon or send away your child because you never know—they may be the one coming back later to save your life. By rejecting you, your grandfather participated in God's plan to give you a wonderful life. So wonderful that you were able to come back and help him. Go love your grandpa, Bamo. And be thankful to God for the wonderful recipe He put together to create your life. Let go of bitterness in exchange for thankfulness. You hear me, son?"

"Yes, Father. I hear you well." Bamo hung up with Chief and went and washed his face. He picked up the phone again. This time he dialed Aunt Namassa.

"Bamo, my son, you've called?"

"Yes, Aunty."

"How are you? I hope you're feeling better since last we met?"

"Yes, Aunty. I'm feeling better."

"Did Krystal tell you that your grandfather is calling for you?"

"Is my grandfather calling for his grandson, or is he calling for the stranger that took him to the hospital?"

Aunt Namassa was silent.

"Aunty, I'm willing to forgive him and my uncles. I'm willing to forgive them from the bottom of my heart. But I'm not willing to play this game and live this lie anymore. I will come to see him, but we must tell him. He must know who I really am."

Aunt Namassa remained silent.

"Aunty?"

"Yes, my son. I hear you. You're right, my son. The thing you have said is correct. We must right the wrong that happened so many years ago." She paused so long that Bamo thought the connection had been lost.

She finally spoke. "It is well. I will talk to Uncle Solo. We will tell your grandfather. And I pray that God touches his heart so he can respond in a way that's proper."

Bamo let out a deep breath.

"Bamo, you know I love you. You are the only child of my dear sister's daughter. They and my mother are all in heaven together. You're all I have left of my dear Diaka. I've only done this to protect you. I saw how hurt your mother was when your grandfather rejected her. I never ever want you to experience that kind of pain in your whole life. Please, you'll forgive me for letting this thing stay for so long? You'll understand that it was only because of my love for you and my love for Diaka?"

Tears streamed down Bamo's face as forgiveness for his aunt flooded his heart. "Yes, Aunty. I understand. Thanks for your love for me all these years and now. You are my mother."

He could hear her choking back tears. "Yes, my son. I am your mother."

Chapter 24

When Bamo, Krystal, Aunt Namassa and Uncle Solo arrived at the compound, they were greeted by Baba and Morris outside of the house. They both had anxious looks on their faces. Their eyes searched Bamo's face, as if they were looking to see how the day would go. They looked as if they were afraid that he was angry.

Bamo gave them a reassuring smile. He wanted to let them know he was fine and that he had forgiven them all for everything. All. But as he had told Aunt Namassa, he wasn't here to pretend to be a friend. He wanted to be introduced as a grandson.

Bamo's grandfather was standing there as they entered the house. Standing strong, smiling and very energetic, walking around with a bob in his step, he looked like a new person as compared to the man Bamo laid eyes on three weeks ago. He shook hands with Bamo. "Young man, you're welcome to my home. Thank you again for everything you've done for me and my family. I am happy to welcome you today."

Bamo showed the sign of respect to an elder by bowing his head while shaking his grandfather's hand.

They all came into the parlor and sat on the old, worn furniture. Bamo eyed the room, thinking of how he would buy all new furniture for his grandfather's house. They sat, and the house girl brought water for everyone to drink. Soon, they moved to the dining table for a grand meal. Bamo knew Baba and Morris had scraped together money for the cassava leaves in palm nut oil and smoked fish with fufu that was being served.

They ate and shared stories of life in Abidjan, politics, sports, and much more. Every few moments in the conversation, Grandpa kept thanking Bamo over and over again. "Son, you're such a good Samaritan. May God bless you for everything you've done for my health."

When the meal was over, per tradition, Grandpa Moussa asked Aunt Namassa and Uncle Solo if they had something to say.

Aunt Namassa replied, "Yes. May we have everyone's attention to hear this news?"

"Before you start," Grandpa Moussa lifted his hand, "I must say in front of everyone, I would like to thank deeply from within my soul this young man, this friend you have brought who has taken interest and care for my life. He came three weeks ago and had me taken to the best hospital in town and got for me the best care. I have never seen this young man, Bamo, until now, but thanks to all of you for him, and I thank him for his attitude and compassion. May God bless you and all your plans for your life." Grandpa Moussa paused for a moment and continued speaking, "Since you saved my life, you deserve many more blessings coming your way and God will clear your path. Thank you so very much. I want you all to join me, to give thanks to him for doing what he's done. Thank you."

Grandpa Moussa concluded his speech and stood to shake Bamo's hand once again. Bamo met his grandpa halfway to secure the handshake as a traditional sign of respect for an elder.

Silence filled the room. There was a tension as everyone seemed to wonder what would come next.

Uncle Solo cleared his throat. "May peace be with all of us."

Everyone nodded.

He continued, "Dear Grandpa Moussa, we address you with all respect due you. There was a situation where all of us were gathered many years ago, twenty-six years ago to be exact. A tragic thing happened to this family all those years ago and I believe

God has brought us around full circle so that the wrong can be righted." Uncle Solo hesitated. "Again, dear Grandpa Moussa, we respect you as the head of this family. You are our father. But many years ago, a decision was made and..." Uncle Solo's voice faltered.

Grandpa Moussa looked at Uncle Solo and looked around the table. "Solo, if we're talking about righting a wrong in the family, is it the correct time while our guest is here? We're here to honor this young man, Bamo, not to settle a family issue. Please, can it keep for another time?"

Uncle Solo paced his words. "This young man, Bamo, is a family issue. Grandpa Moussa..." Uncle Solo looked at Bamo and then back at the elderly man. "This young man, Bamo, who you have called to honor this day. This young man Bamo is..."

He let out a deep breath. "Bamo is your grandson, the son of your daughter Diaka."

Grandpa Moussa gasped and grabbed his chest. He looked at Bamo and stared, his mouth wide open.

Uncle Solo continued telling of Diaka's move to Oume and how she was welcomed there. He told of Bamo's birth, and he paused to speak of Diaka's death. He told of Bamo's trip to America and how well he had succeeded. "And now he's back to continue to be a blessing to Oume and to our nation, Ivory Coast. Grandpa Moussa, this is your grandson, Bamo—son of Diaka, your daughter, daughter of Jeneba, your beloved wife."

Tears had begun streaming down Grandpa Moussa's face when Uncle Solo mentioned Diaka's death. They continued to pour down his face until he finished talking.

Grandpa Moussa moved closer to Bamo and kneeled down beside his chair. His voice was thick was emotion. "My son, my son..." He placed his hands on Bamo's knees.

"Bamo, my son, son of my daughter Diaka..." His voice choked with sobs. He lifted his eyes toward heaven. "My daughter, Diaka. Oh, my daughter. What have I done to you? Daughter of Jeneba, I have wronged you."

Everyone in the room began to shed tears. Grandpa Moussa was shaking as he knelt before Bamo. Baba rose to help his father up from the floor, but Grandpa Moussa waved his hand away.

"Bamo, my son, you must forgive me. I was wrong in the decisions I made toward your mother. God has shown me my wrong, and I regret it. I regret that I sent my daughter away to fend for herself. I regret that you as a son were not born and raised in this house. I'm sorry that I missed my own daughter's funeral." He began to sob again.

Tears poured down Bamo's face. He placed his hand over his grandfather's and squeezed it.

His grandfather put his head down on Bamo's hand. "My son, I don't feel I can live with myself anymore if you deny me as I once denied you and your mother."

He lifted his head and looked at Bamo. "I see that I was too tough with my children. I didn't know how to communicate because that's how I was raised. Most African fathers maintain a mental pressure and toughness on their kids, so they will do well in life and become respectful at all times to themselves and others. But I was wrong. Please, you must forgive me."

Bamo squeezed his grandfather's hand again. "Grandpa Moussa, my father, my grandfather. From the bottom of my heart, I forgive you. God has been in control of my life, and he had made everything turn out for my good and for the good of our whole family. I forgive you. I'm sure my mother in heaven forgives you. I just want us to be a family."

Grandpa Moussa laid his head on Bamo's lap and wept. Bamo leaned down and laid his head on his grandfather's head and cried with him. Everyone in the room was weeping.

Baba finally came and lifted his father from the floor. He sat him in a chair next to Bamo. Grandpa Moussa and Bamo held hands. Krystal stood from where she was sitting and sat down next to Bamo.

Bamo put an arm around her. "Grandpa Moussa, this is my

fiancée, Krystal. She has traveled from America to be with me here in Ivory Coast and to be a part of our family."

Bamo slipped to the floor and knelt in front of his grandfather. "It would honor me so much if you could join us in my village—Diaka's village of Oume—for our wedding in a few weeks."

Grandpa Moussa leaned down to put his head on Bamo's head. He placed his hand on Krystal's cheek. "My daughter, I welcome you. I'm sorry for what you've had to learn of this family, but please see that God is healing us. We are coming together as one. I am honored to welcome you to this country and to our family."

He turned back to Bamo. "I would be honored to be at your wedding."

Bamo stood and pulled his grandfather into an embrace. "You will stand at the wedding as my father. Since I don't know my father, I will be honored for you to be there as my father."

Chapter 25

⚬⚭⚬

Now that things were better with his family, Bamo regretted having scheduled appointments with contractors for the clinic. He wished he had stuck to his original plan of he and Krystal being able to rest and get acclimated to their new surroundings.

They had been having fun, going to restaurants in Abidjan and seeing movies and shopping in some of the nicer shops. Krystal seemed to enjoy bargaining in the market with Aunt Namassa more than she did the fancy shops he had taken her to. He wanted to take her for a weekend trip to the beach, but now he was bogged down with meetings. He kicked himself for letting his anger and bitterness cause him to make a bad decision. It was too late to cancel the meetings, so he had to suffer through them. He had meeting after meeting while Krystal continued to enjoy with Aunt Namassa, shopping, going to the market and cooking Ivorian meals.

Everything was going well in his personal life with Krystal and his family, but business was not so easy. So far, he didn't have any contractor he felt comfortable working with. Many of the companies didn't have much experience with the kind of work he needed done. Others, when he followed up on projects they had done, he could see where they had cut corners and their finished projects had problems.

A contractor that wanted to build their medical clinic gave a great presentation and proposal, but when Bamo went to visit a clinic they had built in Abidjan, all the workers in the building reported problems with construction, water, and electricity. It was clear that money had been pocketed from the contract. Bamo had no interest in working with that kind of company.

He was starting to get discouraged. He didn't want to go with the Chinese company that had submitted a bid to build the clinic, nor a French company. He wanted to be able to do business with and provide jobs for Ivorians, but he had to be sure that the Ivorians would provide quality work and deal with utmost integrity.

He was looking forward to a meeting he had later that afternoon. The company had come highly recommended. This time, Bamo had gone to check on a project this company had completed before the meeting. If he received a bad report, there would be no reason to sit through the meeting.

Bamo tried to remain optimistic as Krystal always encouraged him to be, but he was losing heart. He went to inspect the office building built by KN Enterprises. His optimism was rewarded. He was pleasantly surprised. The building was well built with good finishings. Every worker in the building sang the praises and the owner of the company sang the praises of the contracting company. Bamo was sure this was who he would contract with to build the clinic. If the proposal was good, he was ready to move forward.

Bamo was happy that the CEO of the company had agreed to meet with him. He knew the clinic contract was big money, so they would send a high-ranking manager, but it would be good to meet with the CEO himself. They could negotiate more details without a senior manager having to report back.

The doorbell at the Build Oume office rang, and Bamo opened the door. A tall, dark, lanky man stood there with a smile on his face. His temples, mustache and beard had patches of gray.

"Good afternoon. I'm looking for Bamo Toure of Build Oume?"

"Yes, are you Mr. Nguessan?"

The man nodded. "Yes, Koffi Nguessan of KN Enterprises. Pleased to meet you." Bamo extended his hand. "Pleased to meet you, too. Come in."

Bamo led Mr. Nguessan to their large conference table and took a seat across from him. They stared at each other for a few minutes. Bamo couldn't place it, but something about the man seemed familiar. He couldn't imagine where he would have met him since he hadn't spent any time in Abidjan as he was growing up.

Mr. Nguessan was staring at him as he if was thinking the same thing. "Have we met before?"

Bamo answered. "I don't think so, but you look familiar." He thought maybe he had seen him in a restaurant he and Krystal dined in. It was unsettling.

Mr. Nguessan furrowed his eyebrows. "I must admit that you're much younger than I expected you to be. When I saw the scope of the project, I expected a much more seasoned man. Are you the project director?"

Bamo smiled and nodded. "I am, sir. God has blessed me to accomplish a lot at my age. I schooled in the US and got both my undergrad and masters at Emory University. I worked for two years for one of the largest development companies in the US before moving back home to the Ivory Coast."

In each of the meetings, the CEO's and senior managers had all mentioned how young he was. Bamo found himself running down his resume. He didn't want them to see his youth and think they could take advantage of him.

"Ok, so you are from here. You have an American accent but an Ivorian name so I couldn't be sure. Your face definitely looks like this should be your home."

Mr. Nguessan furrowed his eyebrows again. "Your name sounds familiar. Maybe I went to school with your father or something. What's his name?"

Bamo pursed his lips. "I'm not sure, Mr. Nguessan. I don't know who my father is. Never met the man. He left my mother when she was pregnant."

"Oh, sorry. It's terrible when a man doesn't take care of his child. Very sorry to hear about that."

"It's fine, sir. My life has turned out better than anyone could have ever expected. God has taken good care of me."

Mr. Nguessan looked around the office. Bamo was happy they had decorated the place well and that their surroundings were impressive. This was again, to keep him from being taken advantage of.

"Shall we get started?" Bamo was anxious to hear the company's proposal.

"Yes. I'm really hoping we can end up working together on this clinic project. I'd like to propose several architectural designs with different levels of pricing, and I'll explain the costs and benefits of each. Hopefully, we'll have an option that will work best for you and the people of Oume."

"Sounds good. Looking forward to hear."

They discussed options for more than an hour. Bamo could tell Mr. Nguessan was impressed with the questions he asked. He could tell the man respected him a great deal by the time they finished discussing the details.

"Mr. Nguessan, I have to tell you that I visited two of your building projects and was very impressed with your company's work. I like what you've presented here and will definitely consider your proposal. I have some additional meetings with a few other potential contractors, and then I'll meet with my board before we make a final decision. I hope to finish all of this within the next few weeks. I'm getting married soon and would like to have a signed contract by then."

Mr. Nguessan clapped him on the back. "Congratulations! That's wonderful to hear. You'll marry here in the Ivory Coast?"

"Yes, sir. In Oume. Thank you, sir."

Bamo stood. "Thank so much for taking the time to put together this proposal. If all goes well, I look forward to working with you."

Mr. Nguessan beamed. "I would look forward to that."

Bamo led him to the door. They shook hands.

Mr. Nguessan said, "You're a fine young man, Bamo. I pity your father. He missed out on raising and being proud of the man you've become. I'm sure your mother is very proud."

Bamo bowed his head. "Yes, sir. She watches me from heaven with great joy. She passed away when I was six."

Mr. Nguessan shook his head. "You've lost both your parents and yet you've done so well in life? How is that possible?"

Bamo said, "Only God, sir. Only God."

They shook hands again. Bamo escorted Mr. Nguessan out the door. As soon as he was gone, he called Krystal. "Just met the CEO of KN Enterprises. I think we've got our hospital contractor."

By the end of the next week, Bamo had interviewed a few other contractors for the clinic and was sure he was ready to go with KN Enterprises. He, Krystal and Aunt Namassa needed to travel to Oume to make some plans and decisions for the weddings, so he decided to take the opportunity to have Mr. Nguessan meet him there so they could look at the potential building site for the hospital and get an idea of what they would need to do for water and power.

Krystal and Aunt Namassa scolded him for not waiting until after the wedding to finalize his meetings with Mr. Nguessan, but Bamo knew it would take a while for KN to get him the final numbers after visiting Oume. He wanted the process started so that by the time they returned from their honeymoon in Mauritius, they would be much closer to beginning the clinic project.

Bamo really liked Mr. Nguessan. They had talked a lot on the phone as Mr. Nguessan had come up with other ideas to improve the clinic project. He seemed to be committed to it beyond just business. Bamo appreciated that, and it made him feel like he could trust the man more. They had met again for drinks and had talked and laughed after they finished talking business. The man felt familiar to him for some reason. Mr. Nguessan said the same thing, but they couldn't figure out why.

Bamo, Krystal and Aunt Namassa reached Oume at ten in the morning. They had left early so they could do some wedding things before Mr. Nguessan reached for the meeting at noon. Bamo dropped the two women at the chief's palace to meet with Mama Gnale. They had been chattering about fabrics and menus in the car the whole way. Aunt Namassa was explaining Ivorian traditions while Krystal was sharing the things she wanted to incorporate from her own family's traditions.

Bamo zoned out while the women were discussing women things. He thought about his family and how happy he was that his grandfather would be standing in as his father. He felt a moment of deep sadness that his mother wouldn't be at the wedding. As much as Aunt Namassa loved him and had done for him, and as much as Stephanie loved him, it wasn't the same.

He focused on being grateful for his aunt and Stephanie rather than the fact that his mother wouldn't be there. He thought about Mr. Nguessan's words—that he had turned out to be a fine young man even though he never knew his father and had lost his mother. He could only thank God for that.

After Bamo dropped the women at the palace, he went to his mother's school and sat and watched the students. He realized that this was where his wonderful life had started. He looked around the room at the young children, eager for knowledge, and wondered where they would end up. They could go even further than him, and that thought excited him.

He went back to the Baobab tree where he would meet with Mr. Nguessan and Chief Noumoury to discuss the best site to place the medical clinic. They walked to three potential sites and spent quite some time discussing which would be the best. Bamo could tell that Chief Noumoury really liked Mr. Nguessan just as he did. The three of them chatted easily. Bamo could tell what Chief liked most was Mr. Nguessan's commitment to the project and to improving Oume.

When they finished talking, they all headed back to the palace for lunch. The women were supposed to meet them so they would all eat together. When they arrived, Bamo introduced Mr. Nguessan to Krystal and Mama Gnale. Aunt Namassa had gone to the bathroom. They all went to the parlor area to wait for the cook to finish setting the dining table for their meal.

Aunt Namassa came out to sit with them. Bamo and Mr. Nguessan rose to meet her. He gave her a small bow as a sign of respect for an older woman. Aunt Namassa stared at Mr. Nguessan hard. Her mouth fell open. "Mr. What? What did you say your name was?"

Bamo said, "This is Mr. Koffi Nguessan. He's the CEO of the company that will build our medical clinic."

Aunt Namassa shouted. "My God! Is this true? Could this be true?" She grabbed her head, shouting and shouting, "It cannot be. How can this be? God, is this the way You do your things? Is this the way You cause life to turn?"

"Aunty, what is it? What's wrong?" Bamo looked confused. He felt a little embarrassed by all the emotion she was displaying. This was not like her.

"My God, my God," was all she would say. She paced around the parlor for a few minutes. Everyone stood watching her, wondering what was happening. Mr. Nguessan kept staring at her as if he knew her but couldn't figure out from where.

Chief Noumoury finally grabbed her by the shoulders. "Sister Namassa, what is it? What is bothering you? Please calm down and tell us what is happening."

Aunt Namassa looked at Mr. Nguessan and then looked at Bamo and then looked at the chief. "This is a very strange day and a very strange thing God has done. Please, Chief Noumoury, you'll allow me to talk to you and Mama Gnale in private?"

They quickly bustled away into one of the other grand parlors in the house, leaving Krystal, Bamo, and Mr. Nguessan sitting in uncomfortable silence, trying to figure out what was going on. Finally, Chief's assistant came and asked Mr. Nguessan to join Chief and the others in the other parlor.

Now Bamo was completely confused. What in the world was happening? What had upset his aunt about Mr. Nguessan and why did it require a private conference with everyone but him?

He became more and more agitated as he sat. What was going on? Was this going to affect his contract for the clinic? With the way his aunt had reacted, he knew it must be really bad.

Bamo knew it was wrong, but he wanted to do something he used to do as a young child, growing up in the chief's palace. Private meetings to settle disputes and serious problems were always held in the same parlor they were meeting in now. As a young boy, Bamo had found a sound tunnel between that parlor and one of the guest bedrooms that was hardly ever used.

"Krystal, I'll be right back. I need to go...check on something." Bamo went to the guest bedroom to hear what was going on.

When he entered the room, he heard Aunt Namassa shouting. At first, he couldn't figure out what she was saying. She was shouting and crying at the same time and not making much sense. He finally heard Mama Gnale calming her down. Her shouting reduced to sobs. Bamo was shocked to hear what she was sobbing.

"My Diaka, my poor Diaka." She wailed as she called his mother's name. What did his mother have to do with Mr. Nguessan? Bamo heard the chief's voice.

"Mr. Nguessan, when you abandoned Diaka and fired her from her job, she went through a terrible time and ended up in this village. We took her in as our own. Her child was born here, and this village raised him with her as one family. Diaka died when her son was six. He lived with many mothers in this village. He eventually came to live with me and became my son."

Bamo doubled over when he heard the chief say, "Mr. Nguessan, that fine young man, Bamo, is your son. The son of Diaka, the woman you refused. Bamo is your son."

He heard Aunt Namassa wail and shout again. Bamo staggered

across the room, clutching his chest. He gathered strength and ran out the door. He kept running—past Krystal, out the front door of the palace, past the Baobab tree. Bamo kept running until he couldn't run anymore.

Chapter 26

Bamo found himself at his huge tree, deep in the forest near the river. It was the place he had run to after his mother died. It was there that he ran when he had trouble in one of his many families growing up, and any time he was upset.

Mr. Nguessan was his father? His father? He had a father. Bamo's mind was spinning in contorted circles. It was hard to believe he actually had a father. In his mind, the man was always a ghost—a mystical figure made of smoke. His mother had never talked of his father. She only ever said that Oume village was his father, Chief was his father and God was his father. Jason had become a father to him when he moved to America, but Mr. Nguessan was his flesh and blood father. His father was no longer mystical smoke, but a flesh and blood man. The man's face materialized in his mind.

That was why the man looked so familiar. Looking at Mr. Nguessan was like looking at himself. Bamo didn't look like any of his family members he'd been interacting with over the past month. It troubled him some, and not that he hadn't guessed it, but now he knew why for sure. Baba and Morris looked like Grandpa Moussa. He noted that day at dinner, they had his mannerisms—his smile, his walk, his everything.

Bamo was left-handed, like Mr. Nguessan. They had the same long face with a strong jawline, the same long, lanky frame, and the same rich smile. When he watched Mr. Nguessan walk down the pathway to his car on the first day they met, even his walk looked familiar.

The man was familiar because they had the same DNA.

Bamo shook his head to try to steady his spinning thoughts. He was breathing so fast he was becoming dizzy. He gripped his head between his hands.

This man was his father. He thought of Aunt Namassa's story of how his father rejected his mother. Had been dating her and romancing her and then the minute he found out she was pregnant, he denied her. He'd shamed her in his office, fired her, and sent her away to be disowned by her father.

The man never knew he had a son. Never knew the woman he had impregnated had died. Never knew whether his son was fine or not—well taken care of or not. How could a man even imagine that he had a child somewhere and not wonder if that child was eating, schooling, being cared for in a good way or being abused? How could a man know that a piece of himself was living and breathing in the world somewhere and not wonder how that piece of himself was faring?

Wasn't it a man's job to protect, provide for, and guide his child? How does a man forget his own child?

Bamo didn't realize he was screaming these questions to the tree standing in front of him until he was standing there panting and staring at the tree as if he expected it to answer.

First, it was his grandfather, disowning his mother and not caring about the outcome of his daughter and grandchild. Now, it was his father who disowned his own seed before he was ever born and never once thought about how his life turned out.

It had taken everything in him to forgive his grandfather. He had nothing left for his father.

"I will never forgive you!" Bamo yelled. He punched the tree hard then fell to the ground, grabbing his hand, and howling in pain. He howled and screamed and cried and rolled on the ground for what felt like an hour. Then he just lay there, smelling the fresh earth, staring up at his tree and listening to the river.

His family life was a disgrace. He was disowned by his grandfather, his mother was dead, and now he was meeting a successful man who rejected him in the womb. How could he marry Krystal? How could he ask her to join such a family? It was an embarrassment.

She had a beautiful family with two wonderful parents who married when they were twenty-one and had stayed married all these years. Her older sister was a schoolteacher. Her older brother was a doctor and her younger brother was a missionary and minister like his parents. Krystal had seven nieces and nephews. She kept a big picture of her whole family on the wall in her parlor. Bamo had stared at it many times, looking at beautiful family, seeing their closeness and observing how all the faces resembled each other. How all their eyes were filled with joy and love because they belonged to something amazing. They belonged to each other.

Bamo sat up. Had his father ever married? Did he have brothers and sisters? Bamo's breath hitched again at the thought. Did he have siblings out there that he'd never met before? Did he have nieces and nephews?

After the meeting at his grandfather's house, his family had gathered at Grandpa Moussa's house for another dinner. Uncle Baba had brought his wife, son, and daughter. Uncle Morris had brought his wife and two sons, but it felt strange to Bamo. His cousins were all in their late teens, and he had never met them before.

Did he have brothers and sisters and nieces and nephews right here in this country he had never met before? He was sure he had many aunts, uncles and cousins—members of Mr. Nguessan's family he had never met. Would they all feel like familiar strangers like Mr. Nguessan had?

It was all too much for Bamo. He curled up on his side. He knew he should be concerned about a viper or other wild animals out here in the forest, but he didn't care. No one would find him because no one knew of his hiding spot so he could stay there for hours, waiting for his thoughts to settle.

He didn't want Krystal and Chief and the others to worry, but he couldn't go back just yet. He couldn't face Mr. Nguessan. He was afraid he would punch the man, like he had punched the tree, or maybe he would scream at him about being such an irresponsible man, or maybe even yet, he would fall at his feet, crying like a little boy, asking to be accepted by his father.

Bamo couldn't trust his emotions if he saw Mr. Nguessan face-to-face, so he stay there on the ground, hoping his twisting and turning thoughts would settle.

After a few more moments of staring at his tree, Bamo heard a branch break. He jumped up and moved toward the tree. If it was a wild animal, he was sure he could still climb up it.

Then he heard Chief's voice. "Bamo, where are you?"

A few minutes later, his chief father appeared in the small clearing.

"Bamo..." Chief stood for a few moments to catch his breath. He had obviously run all the way to where Bamo was.

"How did you know where I was? How do you know this place?"

Chief Noumoury smiled while still catching his breath. "Son, how could I not know this place? That first time, when you were young and got upset that Aunt Namassa wanted to take you back to Abidjan, you disappeared for two days. We didn't know where you were. You could have been killed. After that, I told my chief steward to keep a close eye on you and never to let anything happen to the son of Diaka."

"The next time you got upset and ran, he followed you. He stayed out here the whole night, watching over you and then followed you back to the village the next day. Any time you were out here, he was watching you, making sure no harm came to you. I couldn't allow anything to happen to the son of Diaka."

Tears fell from Bamo's eyes.

"I was always your father, Bamo. It doesn't matter what that man Koffi did or didn't do. I was always your father, watching over you, taking care of you, making sure nothing happened to you. I only turned you over to Jason and Stephanie because I knew they could give you a world I couldn't, but I was always and will always be your father."

Bamo fell into his arms and wept. "I know, Father Chief. I know."

As Bamo wept, he felt the anger draining from his body. Once again, he let go of his grandfather, and then he let go of this man, Koffi Nguessan. The man that he looked like and walked like. The man whose DNA filled his every cell. It didn't matter what the man had done or not done. God made sure Bamo had a father.

"Let's go back to the palace. Krystal and your aunt are there worrying over you."

Bamo hesitated. "Mr. Nguessan is still there?"

"Yes, Bamo. He wants to beg your forgiveness." Chief smiled. "Your aunt has cursed him with every curse possible. I actually pitied the man. He has cried and begged. He has begged for your aunt's forgiveness, your precious mother's—may she continue to rest in peace—forgiveness and even though your aunt has abused him, he is waiting to ask for your forgiveness. He refused to leave the palace until you at least hear him."

Bamo bit his lip. He no longer felt angry and didn't want to punch the man. But he didn't want to see him either.

"Remember that your life is from God's perfect recipe," Chief Noumoury said.

Bamo nodded. "Yes, sir."

"How much more so now does that apply with this situation?"

Bamo thought for a second. "My life is God's perfect recipe. My father only played his part in working out God's perfect recipe for my life."

They walked back to the palace together.

When they entered the parlor, the others were sitting there quietly. Mr. Nguessan's eyes were bloodshot red, and he was staring into space. When Bamo entered the room, he leapt to his feet and rushed over to him.

His words came out hurried and garbled. Bamo had no idea what he was trying to say. The man finally fell at his feet, weeping and still speaking. Bamo finally understood as the man said, "I'm so sorry. My son, I'm so sorry."

Bamo knelt down and lifted him from the ground. He didn't really know what to say.

Mr. Nguessan took a deep breath and finally spoke words that made sense. "I was a very foolish young man back then. Very young and very foolish. I was so irresponsible. It's only as I've gotten older that by God's grace, I realized the error of my ways."

He put a hand on Bamo's shoulder. "All I can ask is that you forgive me for being a foolish boy when I was...with your mother. If I could change everything, I would."

Bamo nodded. "I hear you. I can't say that I understand, but I hear you. And I do..." Bamo paused and let out a deep breath. He looked Mr. Nguessan straight in the eye. "I do forgive you." A weight lifted off his chest as he uttered those words.

Mr. Nguessan fell at his feet again, weeping. "Thank you. Thank you, my son. Thank you for finding it within your heart to forgive me."

Bamo knelt down to lift him up off the ground again. It felt uncomfortable having a grown man weeping at his feet. He shook Mr. Nguessan's hand. He didn't feel comfortable embracing him. In fact, he had felt more comfortable with the man before knowing he was his father.

They sat down in uncomfortable silence for a while. Bamo was tired. He wanted Mr. Nguessan to go ahead and leave so he could retreat to his mother's house near the Baobab tree. He wanted to be within its cool walls, thinking of her and feeling her. So much had happened and now he understood everything she had gone through to bring him into the world and to give him the life she had given him.

Mr. Nguessan pulled out his phone. He spoke slowly and hesitantly, as if he was afraid that Bamo would revoke his forgiveness and explode in anger. "Bamo, can I show you something?" He pulled out his phone and started touching the screen.

He held it out to Bamo. "Like I said, I was foolish as a youth, but then I finally grew up. I got married and I have three children." He took a deep breath. "Bamo, you have two brothers and a sister."

Bamo stared at the phone. He was almost afraid to take it and look.

Mr. Nguessan shoved it into his hands. "Please. Look at your brothers and sister."

Bamo looked down at the phone. In the picture, Mr. Nguessan was standing next to a beautiful woman, almost as tall as him. There were three children.

Mr. Nguessan moved a little closer to Bamo on the couch. He pointed at the picture. "That's Mark. He's nineteen. Edmond is seventeen and our princess, Elizabeth, is fifteen."

Bamo didn't even know what to think. Mark could be his twin. He looked exactly like his father and therefore exactly like Bamo. The middle son looked exactly like his mother. The girl, Bamo's sister, looked like a mixture of both parents. His sister. Bamo had two brothers and a sister. It was hard for his mind to absorb. Before he could stop them, words came out of his mouth. "Can I meet them, please?"

Mr. Nguessan laughed. "Of course. Of course. Soonest. However, whenever and wherever. I'll make sure it happens."

Bamo nodded. Yes, he definitely wanted to meet his brothers and sister.

"Can they come to the wedding?"

A tear streamed down Mr. Nguessan's face. "Yes. They can come. I'll bring them. I would love that very much."

Bamo stood. He'd had enough for today. "Mr. Nguessan, Mama Gnale will give you all the details for the wedding. We'll make sure your whole family is well accommodated during your stay in Oume." He didn't know what else to say. He wasn't even sure how he felt about everything. He turned to everyone else in the room. "I'm going to my mother's house now. I need to be...there..."

He leaned down to kiss Krystal on the cheek and whispered in her ear. "I'll be back. I just need a little time. I'll be fine."

She nodded and reached out to squeeze his hand.

Nobody else said a word as he left the palace. Bamo expected to still feel that tortuous mix of emotions but instead, as he entered his mother's home, all he felt was peace. He walked through it, touching the walls, calling her name. He finally lay down on the mattress and fell into a dreamless sleep.

Chapter 27

The week of the wedding had finally come. Bamo, Krystal, and Aunt Namassa spent the week in the village, helping with the final preparations. They left a few days before the wedding for a big trip to the airport. They coordinated things so all their guests would arrive on the same day within hours of one another.

Femi and Chuks had come from Atlanta with Stephanie and Jason to serve as groomsmen. Krystal's parents and her older sister arrived a few hours later. Unfortunately, her brothers weren't able to come, but Krystal was excited to have her best friend from childhood, Lisa, in the wedding party. She came to serve as her maid of honor. Muthoni from their study group and another friend of Krystal's from Emory had come to serve as bridesmaids.

Caleb had flown in from England and was to be Bamo's best man. The two men were so happy to see each other, they just kept slapping hands and hugging each other in the airport.

They all piled into a large van that had been rented for the occasion and headed to Bamo and Krystal's house in Abidjan. Krystal's family and Jason and Stephanie would stay there and in the Build Oume guestroom. The rest of the wedding party would stay at a nearby hotel. The whole group would head to Oume after a good night's sleep.

In Oume, some would stay at Chief Noumoury's palace while others would stay in the chief's palace of the neighboring village. With the exception of Caleb, Bamo didn't think any of their visitors would be comfortable staying in a mud house.

The week before their guests arrived, Krystal had spent many days with the women of Oume village. It was tradition that they would teach her how to be a good wife and member of their community. She was taught how to greet the men and women in the village, how to cook Oume's traditional dishes, and how to interact with men and women in the village with proper respect. They taught her about religion, about the sounds of the drums and what each beat of the drum meant. She also learned about traditional events, weddings, and other ceremonial events.

She learned that the woman is the most important person and has a very important place and role in the family, and how important her input was in her husband's decisions concerning certain issues. She was counseled on how to communicate with her husband first concerning issues, but also knew she could come to the village at any time to talk with the mothers of the village.

Krystal recounted her week to Bamo, mentioning how overwhelming everything was and how beautiful it felt to be welcomed into their community.

Bamo had the same experience. It was tradition for Bamo to spend the week with the elder men of the village. He received counseling on how to handle problems in the marriage and how to ask for help whenever he needed it. He was also advised to allow his wife to come to the village to seek advice from the mothers of the village whenever she needed it.

They counseled him on how to be very sensitive to his wife because most women are fragile compared to men and that even though a man always has to stay in control of his family, he should always listen to his wife and give her the power over the family, even though he was king of his home.

Bamo and Krystal discussed everything they had been counseled on and decided how to incorporate it into the values they already had for themselves.

The day of the wedding was the most beautiful thing they had ever experienced. Bamo had only been minimally involved in the planning, so he wasn't sure what to expect.

He was in his mother's hut, waiting for his father—it was still difficult for him to call Mr. Nguessan that—to come and get him. He had debated long and hard about how much the man should be involved in his wedding ceremony. But one day, Mr. Nguessan called, saying that if Bamo was ready, he would bring his brothers and sister over to visit. They had come to the house. It had been a most beautiful reunion for Bamo. His heart had burst when he stood face to face with his brother, who looked even more like him than they both looked like their father. It was like looking into a mirror.

Bamo couldn't have guessed their first meeting would go so well. Another day, he and Krystal went to their house for dinner and he met his stepmother. She welcomed him with a quiet, sweet spirit and none of the resentment he had feared. After the meal, she and Krystal went into the kitchen to discuss and Bamo had talked for hours with Koffi—as he had insisted Bamo call him if he couldn't call him father.

In that evening, somehow, they regained and even surpassed the level of comfortability they'd had before that terrible day in Oume. Bamo knew that over time, their relationship bond would continue to grow stronger.

After that day, he knew it would be Koffi that would come to fetch him from his mother's house to escort him to the wedding. Koffi adjusted the collar of Bamo's outfit and straightened his hat. Bamo was wearing a traditional, white African wedding garment with lots of intricate embroidery and a wedding hat to match.

Caleb, Femi and Chuks were there in his mother's house ready to march to the wedding with him. They were dressed in similar white, traditional African garments with beautiful embroidery and hats to match. They looked like young African kings. As his mother's house was right across from the Baobab tree, where the wedding was being held, their walk was short. A small boy from the village was dressed in a traditional African outfit that matched the older men. He was to serve as the ring bearer.

The drums began to beat wildly. The people cheered. A bell

rang to signal Koffi that it was time to usher Bamo to his wedding. As Bamo approached the clearing around the Baobab tree, his breath caught at the sight. Koffi's company had built a stage two feet off the ground that was decorated with a beautiful carpet with a runner leading down a path towards the tree. The entire stage and all the chairs on it were decorated with elegant Kente cloth and other African fabrics. There were flowers and natural plants everywhere. He had never seen anything so beautiful.

In the center of the stage, there was a small couch that he knew was for he and Krystal to sit on during the ceremony. It was decorated with Kente cloth and white flower petals.

Bamo's chest was bursting as he saw his grandfather, regally dressed in a long, thick traditional African boubou, typical for an elder. Bamo knew he had never worn anything so regal in all his life. He was sitting in a seat of honor on the stage. Aunt Namassa and Uncle Solo were beside him. Chief Noumoury was seated in front in a traditional gold chief dress well decorated with jewelry and a traditional black leather chief hat. He was carrying an elaborately sculpted wood cane. Mama Gnale was dressed in a royal gold dress with a large head wrap and looked nothing less than a queen.

Jason and Stephanie sat next to Chief and Mama Gnale. They were dressed in matching white African outfits with gold embroidery. Stephanie's face was red and splotchy. Bamo knew she had been crying.

Krystal's mother was there on stage, dressed in a gold African gown with intricate embroidery. He knew Krystal's father was at the chief's palace and would bring Krystal at the designated time in the ceremony.

All of Bamo's mothers that had raised him lined the back of the stage. Their dresses were all designed from the same fabric and they were glowing beautifully, watching with love and pride as Bamo walked from the edge of the clearing toward the stage.

Koffi walked proudly beside Bamo, followed by Caleb, Femi, Chuks, and Jason. All eyes were on Bamo until he reached the stage. After he got there, he scanned the crowd. The crowd was going crazy, shouting his name, "Bamo, Bamo!!!" The drummer was beating even harder.

Bamo was happy to see his stepmother and his brothers and sisters sitting on the front row, along with Baba and Morris and their families and Aunt Namassa and Uncle Solo's children. Krystal's sister was sitting with them, happy for her sister to see this day.

The entire area around the Baobab tree was packed with people, more than Bamo had ever seen before. He was honored that, so many people came to celebrate his special day.

The lead drummer started beating again and Bamo's heart started beating at a rapid pace right alongside the drums. He knew the moment he was waiting for was approaching.

Two small girls from Oume, dressed in colorful African sundresses, carried weaved baskets full of white petals. The crowd laughed as they meandered down the path, throwing flowers everywhere. They were clearly excited about their role in the wedding.

Krystal's bridesmaids—Aicha, her best friend in the US, and one of their classmates from the study group—appeared at the end of the path, wearing elegant gold silk sundresses and adorned in African jewelry. They had been brought by Bamo's decorated truck.

The drum roll started again very quietly and increased in fervor. There was a whole drum troupe from Oume and the surrounding villages, all adorned in their traditional African celebration attire. The traditional whistle blowers followed as the drumroll ended. The tribal whistle signaled the entrance of the bride.

The sounds from the drums and whistles alternated and then played together. The harmony of the whistle and the drums was incredible as the excitement mounted.

The drumroll got very loud and then stopped suddenly. The crowd quieted, and the shofar was blown three times by a native of Oume to announce the arrival of the bride. As the sound of the shofar faded, Krystal descended from a traditional carriage decorated for the occasion. Her father escorted her to the edge of the path.

It felt like Bamo's heart was in his throat. Krystal was glowing in her traditional, embroidered white African wedding gown and the traditional veil. The veil couldn't hide her radiant, sunshiny smile. Her father led her down the path toward the stage.

Tears streamed down Bamo's face. How and why God had blessed him with such a beautiful woman, he would never understand.

As Krystal neared, he could see that her forearms and hands were decorated with blue wedding tattoos. Her father was wearing a white and gold traditional African boubou that matched his wife's gown.

By the time Krystal reached him on the stage, Bamo was completely breathless. He understood why some men fainted at their own wedding. Gazing at her beauty, he felt lightheaded enough to pass out.

The pastor started talking, but Bamo could hardly hear what he was saying. Krystal nudged him and mouthed, "Your vows," laughing at his confusion. They had written and memorized vows to say to each other. Bamo took Krystal's hand.

"I, Bamo, make this promise in the presence of all the eyes here today in Oume. To my beautiful bride and best friend, Krystal, I pledge to love and lead you, to cherish and caress you, to protect and provide for you. I will always be there for you, to guide and grow with you, to direct and dance with you, to cuddle and cleave to you, to satisfy and speak life to you, to share my dreams and spend time with you, to unwrap the gift in you and bring out the very best in you. I care deeply for you, and I will express my love for you clearly and do anything in the world for you. You are the only woman for me. I promise to surrender my heart to you completely from this day forward until death do us part. To you, Krystal, my promise will never be broken."

It was Krystal's turn. "I, Krystal, take you, Bamo, to be my sacred soulmate. I promise to love and to lean on you, to adore and appreciate you, to love and laugh with you, to ignite and inspire you, to uplift and uphold you, to believe in you and build you. I will passionately promote you, treasure and trust you, honor and help you, revere and respect you. I vow to share and surrender my heart to you, to heed and be in harmony with you, to provide and pray for you, to forgive and have fun with you, to spoil you spontaneously, and to write love songs and sweet melodies with you, to fall deeper and deeper in love with you, to delve into deeper depths and to climb to higher heights with you, to speak and move mountains for you and to sail the oceans with you. Thank you for reserving your heart for me only. You are the man God fearfully and wonderfully made just for me. I promise to love you from this day forward as long as we both shall live."

Bamo felt drunk after hearing her words. The lightheadedness continued as they exchanged rings. When it was finally time for Bamo to lift the veil and kiss his bride, kiss her he did. The whole crowd of guests went wild with cheers and shouts.

The pastor announced, "I now present to you, Mr. and Mrs. Bamo Toure."

The crowd cheered as the drum beating restarted. The wedding party began their processional from the stage to the reception area not too far from the Baobab tree where they had cleared and cleaned for the occasion.

The path from the wedding stage to the reception area was lined with skilled traditional drummers, dancers and tribal whistle blowers. The wedding party danced the whole way to the reception tables.

The reception area was filled with many large tables decorated with white cloths, African fabric table runners, and white flower petals. At one corner of the reception area was a beautifully decorated table with the wedding cake.

It took them almost an hour to take all the wedding photos and get everyone was seated.

Chief Noumoury opened the reception with a speech.

"Today my heart is fulfilled. Gnale and I and the entire village of Oume are extremely happy to see Bamo and his wife happily joined in marriage. This is a day that his mother, Diaka, would have been extremely proud of. She was very special to us here in Oume, and my wife and all the village mothers in Oume stand proudly in her place. We are all very proud of Bamo. He has grown up to be a sincere, respectful, and humble young man. He has his mother's heart of compassion and kindness. He has made the whole village and his family proud of him. When Namassa brought his mother Diaka here to Oume, none of us knew it, but they were bringing new life to Oume. We poured our kindness on Diaka, then she poured out love and kindness on this village and gave her life for its welfare. She gave life to Bamo, and now Bamo has given life and love back to Oume. God has blessed us for blessing Diaka and has blessed Diaka by blessing Bamo. It's a beautiful circle of love and blessing."

The crowd cheered.

Chief finished his speech by saying, "May God continue to bless Bamo with the love of this beautiful woman He has given her. May they enjoy a rich deep love and a beautiful long life. May God be with them always. Oume will always love you and pray for you that you would experience the life, love and blessings that God has reserved for you."

Bamo leaned in and kissed Krystal. Everyone clapped.

The reception ceremony continued with other speeches and blessings and finally the Master of Ceremony announced, "Ladies and gentlemen, this is the climax of their wedding celebration. It's time for the jumping of the broom!"

Everyone cheered. Krystal and her family and the other US visitors were excited to see something in Africa that they had only heard about in their country.

The Master of Ceremony explained, "The jumping of the broom symbolizes the couple's new beginning and that they would be together for life. In the moment they jump the broom, they are entering the door to their new life together forever. After they jump, they are in unity and harmony to overcome every obstacle to remain together for life. We are so happy to witness and share this special moment with them."

Bamo and Krystal rose and came from behind the head table to an area in front. Caleb came forward and laid the broom on the ground in front of them. The maid of honor took her place behind Krystal to hold her wedding train. The crowd was extremely quiet, waiting in anticipation for the moment.

The Master of Ceremony said, "And now, ladies and gentlemen, at the count of three..."

The crowd counted to three, and Krystal and Bamo jumped. Everybody cheered, and Bamo leaned over and kissed Krystal on the mouth. He didn't care about being modest in front of his family anymore. He was a married man.

The rest of the wedding reception included much eating, drinking and a whole night of dancing. Bamo and Krystal danced themselves into happy exhaustion and then made the rounds at the reception, greeting all their guests. Everyone wanted their chance to hug them, bless them, and wish them well.

When everything was over, Bamo and Krystal retreated away from the crowd. Bamo was full of joy as he escorted his bride to his mother's house.

Bamo was concerned about Krystal sleeping in the mud hut instead of Chief's palace, but when he asked her about it, she said, "Bamo Toure, there's no other place I would rather spend my first night as your wife."

Epilogue

∾

A little less than a year later, Krystal gave birth to a baby girl. Krystal and Bamo never had to think about what to name her. The choice was easy—their baby girl's name was Diaka.

Life was good in Abidjan. The medical clinic was halfway done, and Bamo took frequent trips to Oume with his father, Koffi, to check on its progress.

They were still in slow meetings with the government and village chiefs about the levy project. There was so much corruption and argument about who would get what money. Bamo could only hope there was no more flooding and that no lives were lost before everything was resolved and the levies were built.

When Baby Diaka was about eight months old, they took her to Oume for her naming ceremony and birth celebration. Krystal had wanted the baby's immune system to develop a little before she traveled to the village for the first time. Everyone in the village kept asking when they would come, and Bamo kept making excuses for why it was taking so long.

Bamo finally convinced Krystal that the water system they had installed in the village was safe for their daughter and that they would take precautions to make sure she didn't get malaria. Krystal was willing to expose herself to anything in their new home in Africa, but she was very protective of their daughter.

Finally, the day came for them to travel to Oume, and Bamo was excited to introduce Baby Diaka to his mother's village. They packed the truck with everything they would need for the journey and set out for the six-hour trip.

When they reached the outskirts of Oume, they couldn't make it anywhere near the village before their truck was swarmed with children, Bamo's mothers and friends wanting to get a first glance at Baby Diaka. They sang her name as Bamo and Krystal walked her into the village. When they finally ended at Mama Diaka's house, Bamo was overcome. To be able to bring baby girl Diaka to his mother Diaka's house was an incredible, full circle moment and he could barely handle the thought.

Early in the morning of the next day, Mama Gnale and her team and all Bamo's mothers organized a huge celebration for Baby Diaka under the Baobab tree. She was passed through all of Bamo's mothers until she finally landed in the arms of Mama Gnale. The chief took her and lifted her up toward heaven, pronouncing a long blessing over her.

Mama Gnale and all Bamo's mothers cried through most of the ceremony. Aicha was there crying right along with them.

There was a huge feast under the Baobab tree after the ceremony was over. Baby Diaka was passed from person to person until finally Krystal started fussing and took her baby. She didn't want her to get sick from so many people holding her.

That night after the ceremony, Krystal and Bamo fell exhausted on the thick queen mattress set on top of a decorative wood frame he had bought for Krystal for when they slept in the house. He wasn't going to have his wife sleeping on a thin foam mattress on the floor, no matter how much she asserted that she had grown up as a missionary.

They both fell asleep almost as soon as their heads hit the pillow with Baby Diaka sleeping between them. Bamo wasn't sleeping for long when he heard his daughter crying. He couldn't believe he had a beautiful daughter. She looked just like her mother.

He was surprised Krystal didn't wake up, but he knew she was exhausted from the trip and all the festivities. He wanted his wife to rest, so he picked up the baby and took her into the other room.

He paced back and forth with her, but she continued to cry. Bamo didn't think she was hungry. Krystal had fed her before they all went to sleep.

"Baby Diaka, what's wrong, eh? What's wrong with Daddy's baby girl?"

He held her against his chest. She leaned back and touched the necklace hanging around his neck.

His mother's necklace. He had taken it from Krystal in exchange for the engagement ring he gave her. Not too long after he proposed, she told him she didn't feel right taking his mother's heirloom, and besides if he wanted her to travel across the ocean with him, he better put a ring on it. He laughed. And then he did.

Since they had come back to the Ivory Coast, he wore his mother's necklace every day.

Baby Diaka pulled on the chain.

Bamo kissed her forehead. "Oh, you want my necklace. In fact, it will be yours one day when the time is proper, but for now I will keep it safe for you."

He nuzzled her into his chest. "Let me tell you the story of this necklace and the woman who wore it before me."

Baby Diaka stopped crying and seemed to be listening to her father's voice.

"Diaka, my daughter, you are a special child and the namesake of an amazing woman who gave me life and gave life to the village of Oume after they gave life to her and to me. I tell you now the legacy of your grandmother Diaka."

Bamo whispered into his daughter's ear the story of his mother's life. His heart was filled with pride as he did so. He talked and walked for a while, telling his daughter the story of strength, resilience, and love. She finally fell asleep on his chest, but he knew she had absorbed the story into her little soul.

He finished by saying, "Your grandmother, Diaka, was a very strong woman. A beautifully strong woman, as you will be one day."

About the Author

Keleti Sanon considers himself to be a man on a mission to connect Africa to the rest of the world. He is a best-selling author whose passion as a writer is in sharing the beauty, culture, and history of his homeland in Abidjan, Ivory Coast. In his first book, *Another Change Maybe the Last* (Oct 2009), he explores the complex issues and strained relationships between people of the African diaspora and offer hope and solutions for restoration.

In his second published work, *The Adventures of Bamo* (August 2019), readers meet fictional characters, Diaka and Bamo Toure. The story begins in Abidjan, Ivory Coast, and then takes readers on an immersive journey through small village life in Oume, Africa to urban life in the United States. The Adventures of Bamo embodies the virtue in the African proverb: It take a village to raise a child.

In addition to his work as an author, Keleti holds two college degrees and has enjoyed a successful 20-year career as professional aircraft mechanic. He resides in Humble, Texas, USA. Visit him at www.KeletiSanon.com